T0279728

THE INVISIBLE

SELF

Broken Childhood, Primal healing

by

Michelle Taja Miller

The Invisible Self / Michelle Taja Miller
ISBN: 979-8-9902596-0-7
Library Of Congress Registration Number
TXu 2-397-482
© Cover Design by Michelle Taja Miller

For André

Foreword

I started Primal Therapy at the Almont Clinic in 1970 when I was 25 years of age. Despite initial challenges, my early experience of the feeling process validated the Primal therapeutic approach, revealing the origin of, contradicting and helping me overcome my deepest inner beliefs of unworthiness and shame. I persisted, entered training, and eventually became a Certified Primal Therapist. From 1989 to 1995, I ran Art's new Primal Training Center in Venice, California and since then, I've had my own practice in West Hollywood, California.

I met Michelle when she joined the training program I supervised. She is one of the few people I have known who has an intuitive understanding of Primal therapy; it is a rare quality.

In the pages that follow, Michelle relates her formative experiences, many of which were devastating. Despite the challenges she would later face, early bonding with her father gave her the foundation of acceptance and security, however brief, which I have come to believe is crucial to success in therapy. She remained intact and retained her empathy, avoiding the hideous scars of neurosis which disfigure so many of us. In the re-discovery of her repressed trauma, she found insight and peace of mind with lessons for us all.

We follow this paradigm through Michelle's life experiences, both those which nourished her development and those so traumatic that their repression was essential to her survival. And uniquely, she is able to relate the recapture of that repressed material during her therapy and explain how it subconsciously influenced her perceptions, her relationships and indeed the very experience of her life.

These Primal insights are unique, for they come to us after we consciously react to the traumas of our past *for the first time*, so we discover—what was truly driving us - our repressed, and therefore unconscious, response to childhood emotional injury. These insights are the true gift of Primal Therapy — once we have reacted to what's repressed, it becomes just a conscious memory of our history, no longer warping our perceptions and causing us ineffable distress.

Beautifully written, this spellbinding narrative chronicles both her early years and some of her journeys back into the inferno. Although Michelle's life might not fit the standard definition of a "success story," it is nevertheless a triumph of the human spirit over overwhelming adversity and is an inspiration, a beacon of light for a myriad of souls still mired in darkness.

Jonathan Christie

Jonathan S. Christie, MA, MFT, Certified Primal Therapist, and Author of *Foods for Vitality*

Acknowledgments

I want to thank Jonathan Christie for all his support, for patiently reading draft after draft, and for being a trusted mentor who believed in me from the first day we met.

To my friend Penny, for sharing her wonderful command of the English language, and for being a friend at the end of the phone when writer's block had me climbing the walls …

To Andy for his inspiring poetic and creative use of the language in song writing, which inspired me to work harder at becoming a writer.

To my ex-husband, my best friend, Ken who seemed constantly able to extend the boundaries of acceptance and love, and to my friend Peter, a rock of ages, whose support never wavered, an intellectual sparring partner forever challenging my core concepts and beliefs.

Finally, to my cats for their gentle nature, and playful antics that kept me smiling, and who reminded me through my days of turmoil and upheaval that eating and sleeping were non-negotiable.

Introduction

Why did I write my story? *Perhaps* to regain a sense of my own history? Words began to flow, and soon turned into a collection of stories recounting a journey of self-discovery, my fight to survive and to heal. Over the years, my therapeutic journey had helped me connect the dots between my past experiences and my present life struggles. Gradually, I was able to regain a sense of my authentic self and heal the wounds of my childhood traumas.

The therapeutic process had offered me alternative solutions to a life of despair. By uncovering the origins of my panic disorder, fear of abandonment, and relentless search for validation, I uncovered the true story, that of my invisible self.

I came to realize that what I wrote was not solely the journey of my healing; it transcended that. It illustrated how Primal therapy when done right offers hope to others, and I wanted to share that hope, offer inspiration, by showing them that healing is possible and that they are not alone on their journey.

But as I put words down on empty pages, a whisper of doubt remained, because Primal therapy, in its application, has often been in opposition to its own original concepts, as it often failed to provide a nurturing therapeutic environment. Additionally, its flawed implementation that has prevented it from gaining acceptance as a conventional therapeutic method within the psychological community caused me to question its relevance.

However, despite these challenges, I came to recognize its unique ability to alleviate human suffering, by helping individuals access, relive, and resolve deep-seated traumas. The hurdles I encountered did not lead me to reject the therapy, but instead inspired me to find my own path within it.

Its promise goes beyond it. By delving into our unconscious traumas, we are addressing the root causes of societal issues like conflict and environmental degradation, paving the way for a more harmonious existence. This hope for societal transformation fueled my belief in the importance of sharing my experiences and insights, that I view as a contribution towards a brighter future for humanity.

The transformative power of restoring consciousness is undeniable. It enables us to fulfill our potential, it breaks the cycle of perpetual trauma, and prevents its transmission to future generations.

This book is about the recovery of a "self," scarred but healed. I wanted to share my story with the world, in the hope of attracting readers from many walks of life, including midwives, nurses, pediatricians, psychologists, and therapists, all experts in various modalities, with the common goal of helping their patients heal from the devastating effects of early childhood trauma.

Contents

The Story	The Invisible Self	Page 3
	Flashback	Page 3
Chapter One	The Family Heirloom	Page 5
	My Father	Page 10
Chapter Two	Coming Into this World	Page 13
	Reflections & Insights	Page 16
Chapter Three	Family Bliss	Page 19
	Early Losses	Page 23
Chapter Four	Onto Another Foster Home ….	Page 29
Chapter Five	The Red Bucket	Page 35
Chapter Six	The Leaf	Page 41
Chapter Seven	Kicks & Screams	Page 45
	Reflections & Insights	Page 48
Chapter Eight	The Visit	Page 53
	Reflections & Insights	Page 59
Chapter Nine	Monsieur Valcourt's Secret	page 65
	Reflections & Insights	Page 72
Chapter Ten	New Home, New Rules	Page 77
	Reflections & Insights	Page 88
Chapter Eleven	Let Me Help You Breathe	Page 91
	Reflections & Insights	Page 97
	Insights	Page 99
Chapter Twelve	That Old Yearning	Page 103
Chapter Thirteen	Confusion & Misery	Page 107
Chapter Fourteen	The Jerrican	Page 113
	Reflections & Insights	Page 121
	Summer of Peace	Page 123

Chapter Fifteen	Music. A New Lifeline	Page 127
	A Turbulent Year	Page 132
	Reflections & Insights	Page 142
Chapter Sixteen	The Lifeline Breaks	Page 145
Chapter Seventeen	Summer in Israel	Page 155
	Reflections & Insights	Page 165
	Leaving Home	Page 167
Chapter Eighteen	A Brave New Life	Page 171
Chapter Nineteen	A Love Triangle	Page 183
Chapter Twenty	A Weekend in Amsterdam	Page 191
	Panic	Page 195
	Reflections & Insights	Page 197
Chapter Twenty-One	Free Love Comes at a Price	Page 201
Chapter Twenty-Two	Someone Found. Someone Lost	Page 211
Chapter Twenty-Three	Trapped In Trauma	Page 219
	Sleep Therapy	Page 225
	Reflections & Insights	Page 230
Chapter Twenty-Four	Something Old. Something New	Page 235
	Old Memories Emerge	Page 238
	Reflections & Insights	Page 243
	Reflections & Insights	Page 245
	The Gift of Dialectic	Page 252
Chapter Twenty-Five	Leaving France	Page 255
Appendix	Primal Therapy Done Right	Page 259

The Story

I

The Invisible Self

Flashback

FROM TIME TO TIME, friends of Madame Valcourt would come to visit. They would sit at the kitchen table, talking, laughing, and eating. I liked these times so much as Madame Valcourt's attention was elsewhere.

On one afternoon, a woman who had been there before showed up for tea. They sat as usual and spoke loudly, animatedly. I heard a tone in their voices that announced trouble; something in Madame Valcourt's pitch changed almost imperceptibly, but I was in high alert so much of the time that I had learned to detect every nuance in adults' voices.

"This one is a bleeder!" Madame Valcourt exclaimed.

Before I had a chance to turn and run, Madame Valcourt flew toward me, held my shoulder with one hand, and punched me in the face with the other. It was so sudden that my reaction was absolute surprise for a split second, followed by shock. I really did not understand what had just happened or why.

Fierce pain shot from my nose to my cheekbones and my teeth. Then I felt something soaking my face and my clothes.

I stood there like a petrified statue. I could not move; I was just watching the flow of blood running down from my face, dripping onto the tiled floor; then, like in a trance, I felt myself running to the white ceramic sink, and leaned over it, mesmerized as the white surface turned deep red. It was then that I heard the woman's gleeful laugh explode behind me.

"See, I told you she was a bleeder," Madame Valcourt shrieked.

No one came to my rescue. I was holding my face with both hands now, running through the dining room, and out into the garden to a faraway corner where I lay down in the grass, pinching my nose. I looked at the grasses and the trees and the deep gray sky, desperately trying to fix my attention on something, anything. Every few seconds, I would look at my fingers to see if the blood flow had stopped. My heart was beating so fast that I was afraid it was going to jump out of my chest.

I stayed in the garden for a long time, immobile, feeling the blood dry up and crack all over my cheeks. I just lay there until the sky turned dark, not moving, playing dead. Enveloped by the black of the night, I did not feel scared anymore. I hoped that they would forget all about me and that I could stay there just like that forever and ever.

CHAPTER I

The Family Heirloom

MY GRANDMOTHER, Sarina Nahmias was born in Thessaloniki, Greece, in the early 1900s. Her father, Joseph Nahmias, was a wealthy and respected businessman in their community of Sephardic Jews. He cared about his family, but he was not the kind of man to demonstrate affection. As her mother died soon after she was born, Sarina grew up motherless ... and isolated. She had a brother, already a young adult, and a sister in her teens.

Sarina received a first-class education, and by the time she was 18, she was fluent in French in addition to the languages spoken at home: Greek and Ladino, the old Spanish that Sephardic Jews have spoken ever since the Spanish Inquisition sent them fleeing all over Europe. Her education was comprehensive; she learned how to run a household, and how to become an accomplished, well-mannered young woman so that when the time came, she would be considered a suitable wife for a future husband. But Sarina could not wait to run away from the suffocating traditions of her father's home.

In the early part of the twentieth century in Greece, the father chose a husband for his daughters. Marriage was an economic and social arrangement between families. Once married, the woman would take care of the household and give her husband children, preferably boys. Sarina was not a woman who could live such a passionless and dependent life. She was restless, with a fervent longing for adventure. She rejected traditions; she wanted to make her own choices. She cared as little about money as she cared about conventions, so marrying for economic security had no appeal for her.

Sarina married her first husband, Ernest Cohen, for love in defiance of traditions. She bore his child – my mother, Reine – but it was not long before she realized she had rushed into marriage with the wrong man. She was furious to discover that her husband expected her to rein in her rebellious spirit, settle down and become a traditional wife. They fought a lot, two strong personalities up against each other, neither one backing down.

The day came when Sarina had had enough. She took Reine and ran away to a place she had always dreamed of, Paris. She was attracted to this modern, bustling city famous for its artists and revolutionary thinkers. She was driven by a fierce desire to build a life for herself and become an independent woman. Guided by the idealism of youth, she overlooked the practical. She had no income, no job, no contacts in France, and a four-year-old daughter to look after.

In the end, it was her father who came to her rescue. Once he understood that his daughter was beyond his sphere of influence and that she would never return to Greece, he traveled to France to help her get settled. He bought her a small store and the apartment above it. Sarina divorced Ernest and began a new chapter of her life.

Upon her arrival in France, she felt handicapped by the presence of a child she was not equipped to care for. Reine was a burden, an encumbrance, a piece of luggage that had to be stowed away. With no family to help her, my grandmother decided to leave her daughter in the hands of strangers in a foster home until she settled into her new life.

Deserted, Reine had no one to tell how much she missed her father and her home and everyone she'd known back home. She missed hearing the language of her childhood. In the foster home, she was ridiculed for her inability to speak French, for her flamboyant red hair, her freckles. Disoriented and scared, she started wetting her bed, which infuriated the foster mother. Once, as a punishment, Reine was made to walk around the courtyard with the wet sheet on her head in front of a crowd of kids. She told me that story many, many times as she was going from one emotional breakdown to another, one hospital to another, one suicide attempt to another.

While still in Greece, Sarina met Moïse Ventura, who had fallen madly in love with her, so much so that he followed her all the way to Paris, leaving behind parents, siblings, friends, and his professional life. He was a Greek journalist who wrote fiery articles denouncing the repressive Greek regime. Expressing his views had landed him in jail on more than one occasion.

Reine spent a year in foster care before Sarina brought her back to live with her and Moïse, now called Maurice. His old name was dangerously Jewish in the burgeoning antisemitism of prewar Paris.

Maurice loved Reine with all his heart, but he was a dreamer who idealized life and was blind to his wife's flaws. Before long, Sarina was holding the reins. Four years after Reine returned home, her brother Claude was born. Maurice became even more passive and let his wife order him around as if he was a child, which left his children at the mercy of their volatile mother.

In May 1940, after Hitler invaded the north of France, the south was still an unoccupied "Free Zone." At that time, people believed that only men were at risk of being arrested and deported by the Nazis. So, in late 1941, Sarina persuaded her husband to leave Paris and wait out those dangerous times with friends in the Free Zone while she stayed in Paris with five-year-old Claude and fourteen-year-old Reine.

I grew up on tales of those terrible years. My mother and grandmother were haunted by the brutal memories of the occupation. They now lived in the 11th arrondissement, while their store was in the 12th. To go from the apartment to the store, they had to cross the Rue du Faubourg Saint-Antoine that divided the two districts. On a cold winter day, Reine was on her way to the store to help her mother as she usually did. Holding her little brother's hand, she stopped on the curb on the 11th district side to wait for cars to go by so they could safely cross over to the 12th district side. Suddenly, she saw a large group of men come running from every direction. Nazis and pro-Nazi French men surrounded the 12th district and proceeded to arrest every Jew on the street, - men, women, and children - loading them like cattle onto army trucks. Reine could not stop staring at the avenue, terrified by the screams, the tears, the confusion. Had she crossed just seconds earlier, she and her little brother would have been picked up too, never to be heard from again.

A short year after Maurice had taken refuge in the south, the Free Zone was also invaded. The Nazi government imposed mandatory ID badges for Jews: The Star of David, with the word "Juif", (French for "Jewish"), written on it. This was one of the tactics used to isolate Jews from the rest of the population, enabling them to identify, deport, and ultimately exterminate the Jews of Europe.

When the entire country fell under German occupation, Sarina decided that the best thing for her family was to be together. She prepared to leave Paris and rejoin her husband in the south, but as so many were fleeing the city, she only managed to get two tickets. She left with Claude and entrusted friends with her daughter's safe voyage.

My mother never forgot being left behind in the care of "friends" who were strangers to her. She told me that story time and time again, pain written all over her face, tears running down her cheeks. To Reine, this was the ultimate betrayal by her mother and the undeniable proof that Sarina had chosen her son over her. Reine was expendable. My mother never recovered from it, and although she joined her family soon after, her relationship with Sarina was now beyond repair. I could hear the mix of rage and despair in her trembling voice as she spoke. That unexpressed rage turned into hatred, and so my unforgivable grandmother remained unforgiven.

Once the war ended, there was relief, but there was also a void. For years they had lived one day at a time, never knowing what the next day would bring or if they would survive at all. Now that she was free, now that she did have a future, 18-year-old Reine felt adrift, not sure what to aspire to nor what to dream about. She began to attend classes at a Jewish club where young adults would get together. They formed a theater troupe, played music, picnicked in the gardens, and held parties.

During this time, Reine had turned into a beautiful woman. Her friends from the old days said she looked like Rita Hayworth and that the boys were all in love with her. Among her admirers were two people who were to play important roles in my life: my father, and my stepfather.

MY FATHER

My father, Louis Miller, was born in Warsaw, Poland. When he was a boy, his family moved to Belgium, where he grew up. He had an older brother and a younger sister. During the Nazi occupation of Belgium, the entire family survived by hiding in the maid's quarters on the top floor of an apartment building in Brussels, spending years carefully remaining unseen and unheard. After the war, his family moved to Paris.

My father was a talented painter, musician, and an artisan who made leather goods. My mother admired his music and fell in love with him; they married and moved into the apartment just next door to Sarina's. He set up his leather workshop in one of the rooms of the small apartment.

My grandmother was dead set against this marriage right from the start. Ironically, the woman who had once spit in the face of convention and married for love thought little of her new son-in-law because he did not a have steady job with a guaranteed income. She doubted that he could be a good provider for his family. But I always suspected there was more to my grandmother's dislike of her son-in-law. Maybe she was not entirely aware of it, but a certain class snobbery informed her judgment as well. In Thessaloniki, Sarina's family had status and were thought of as royalty within the Sephardic Jewish community, which they generously supported. They often opened their home to feed the poor, especially during times of hardship, such as the infamous fire of 1917, which burnt more than half the homes to the ground.

My grandmother was proud of her heritage and expected her daughter to marry into a well-to-do family. In her eyes, Louis was not from a "good" family or at least not good enough to marry into hers. He was born to a poor family of Ashkenazi Jews. It was no surprise that his charm and artistic talents did not impress Sarina in the slightest.

Hoping to control her daughter's life, my grandmother demanded a key to the newlyweds' apartment. After all, she was paying the rent. From then on, she could walk in and out of it whenever she pleased, invading their privacy, and undermining their intimacy. Sarina was determined to ruin the marriage.

Ignoring his mother-in-law's behavior, Louis, with his good nature and natural optimism, kept working in his small workshop. But Reine's insecurities made her vulnerable to her mother's constant criticism of Louis. She became pregnant almost right after the wedding, but the thought of having a child to take care of was just too much. As time went by, she became more and more frightened; then more and more depressed, and before long she felt so overwhelmed that she attempted suicide in the fourth month of her pregnancy by taking handfuls of sleeping pills. She was taken to the hospital where the doctor pumped her stomach. Although physically she recovered right away, she was still severely depressed. My mother's suicide attempt made my grandmother reconsider her behavior, and she stopped harassing the couple — at least for the time being.

Reine started spending more time with her cousin Rose, now married, and living just one flight of stairs above my parents. They had been best friends since childhood in Greece, and the bond between them was strong despite the many separations. Luckily, Rose's joy about being a mother to Sabine, her beautiful baby girl, was contagious. This helped my mother recover, and by the time spring came around, she felt ready for a new beginning.

CHAPTER II

Coming into This World

AS INFANTS, our brain records everything with our senses, but there are no words, we do not know that it is a window, the sky, a blue color, or a tree, it's all sensory recordings. When repression blocks memories, it blocks what our senses picked up at the time. But as we go back in time, we retrieve these sensory memories, and we now have words. That's how, as the veil of repression lifts, pre-verbal memories can be described retroactively.

The story of my birth comes from my recovered memories, and from my mother's account of the day she gave birth to me.

It was a warm and sunny spring day, and I was due anytime now. *I was an infant in my mother's womb, blissfully bathing in serene peacefulness.*

Wearing her favorite high-heeled shoes, my mother left the apartment, locked the door behind her, and headed down the dark corridor. She started down the wooden staircase, holding on to the banister. Somehow, her foot did not quite land on the next step; she twisted her ankle and lost her balance. For a split second, she watched herself fall in slow motion, but the pain that shot through her body, bouncing against the steps and the intense contractions triggered by her fall, brought her back to the present moment.

Her water broke.

A sudden jolt. Safety turned into chaos; I felt the loss of control and vertigo as my mother's body was tumbling down and I with her. I felt the jolts of adrenaline that shot through her in that long moment of falling. My heart was in sync with hers, pounding faster and faster. Water rushed all around, the tidal wave passed over me.

Dizzying fall down the birth canal, a violent, brutal shock on top of my skull as it banged against something hard. Violent shaking: her body – like the Earth – overpowered by waves of quakes, each more powerful than the last, and for me, the absolute urgency to fight and to survive. Then I'm stuck somewhere, cannot move forward, cannot move backward, cannot stay put. Living the impossible.

Her screams alerted the neighbors who came to her rescue and called an ambulance. Upon her arrival at the hospital, my mother was rushed to the delivery room, and was given oxytocin, inducing violent contractions that threw me into yet another state of futile frenzy, desperately attempting to move forward, held back by the umbilical cord wrapped around my neck, until exhaustion slowly took over.

Contracting muscles all around. Hers? Mine? I've got to get out, I've got to get out. But I can't, I can't. I can't. Living, breathing enemy walls closing in from all directions, my burning skin savagely sanded, pain, fire … soundless screams of fear and rage, useless battling, fighting to the death against my mother, her womb, my home, gone, bombed, collapsed, destroyed, nowhere to go, and slowly letting go, letting go and the calm of death invades. Giving up. Battle over.

And then the cold, rigid blades of the forceps against my skull, pressing hard, pulling me out, to the rescue. Help's here! Grabbed by the feet, flying through the cold air, then the agonizing upside-down fall into emptiness, down and down. Then screaming in terror ...

My body felt like a ship after a brutal storm, damaged, banged up, old well beyond its years.

The sensations and later the emotions, laid upon the imprints of birth, have persisted through my life in girlhood and womanhood at every turn of the road, emerging whenever I felt I was swimming upstream in an unending battle against the currents of life's events.

My mother and I were moved to a large room. It had one of those old-fashioned mosaic floors of asymmetrical tiles, black and brown on white, and a large French window wide open, overlooking a massive, welcoming chestnut tree covered with new, tender green leaves and, behind it, filtered through the leaves, a deep, deep blue sky.

The gentle warmth of the spring afternoon filled the room with a delightful calmness that soothed my tiny, battered body. Oh, how I loved that moment! It was a small twinkling that was going to help me through life's worst storms. Something that shone in the distance, spelling the words *hope* and *light*; a light at the end of the tunnel, a lighthouse guiding the lost sailor back to shore. It was my first moment of pure joy.

My grandmother arrived soon after I was born as my mother was resting in a bed of fresh linens in the sunlit room. She sat down on the chair next to the bed, looked at her daughter and exclaimed, "What are you going to call her, Catastrophe?!"

My mother told me she looked away without a word.

As I am writing this, my grandmother's words come back to me, "Children are a terrible burden; if I could start my life over, I would never have any, ever!" I remember the bitterness in her voice as she spoke. She was disappointed, angry at her own life, her own decisions or lack thereof; her face frozen in an expression of resentment became ever more pronounced as she grew older.

My mother had enduring emotional problems throughout her life, but her own mother showed no warmth, no maternal concern, and had no kind words to alleviate her pain. My grandmother took no responsibility and admitted no guilt as she witnessed Reine's distress. As a girl, I heard her repeat over and over: "What did I do to deserve *this*?" What "this" meant to her was always a mystery to me.

My grandmother had failed her daughter in the most fundamental way: she had failed to provide what any living being needs first and foremost: a mother's love. And history was about to repeat itself, because how can anyone give what they never had?

~ REFLECTIONS & INSIGHTS ~

Many years later in Primal Therapy sessions, understanding exploded like a bright light revealing dark areas in the brain where memories had been hidden. I could see them now, as if for the first time even though I knew they had been there all along. As I re-lived the crushing urgency to escape my mother's womb, pieces of the puzzle fell into place, revealing to me a continuity and logic that made so much sense it left me breathless.

My entire life was a replay of the sequences of my birth, perfectly designed to escape anytime from anywhere and from the memory of its imprints. No wonder I was claustrophobic! No wonder the thought of an elevator or being 'trapped' in an airplane terrified me. I understood now why I had weeks of shattering nightmares about falling, after I saw an earthquake scene in a movie. Horrified, I had watched people running for their lives, and the earth, opening like a giant mouth, swallowing them into oblivion.

I was always anticipating the worst-case scenario, planning accordingly, sitting close to exits wherever I went, on alert, ready to run for my life.

I realized that the panic attacks that descended upon my life in my early twenties were the precise reenactment of the original experience, and these terrifying sensations, a perfect match to the sequences of my birth, my very first experience of ineffable terror, in its exact order but disconnected from the original context.

I also came to understand how sensations of falling and terror would be later compounded by the devastating feelings from the multiple abandonments throughout my childhood, one leading to the other in an endless dance back and forth so that I came to experience abandonment as falling.

But just as the memories of fear and pain came into focus, so did the memories of calm and peaceful well-being because as surely as night follows day, there will be a gentle warmth filling the room with a delightful calmness that soothed my tiny, battered body. So I loved the

17

ending of a warm spring afternoon, the quiet feeling that came over me at the end of each day as the city's frantic activity all around me seemed to calm and quiet down, the silence incomplete, with just enough life out there to still feel connected.

My perennial April escapes to warm faraway countries made so much sense now. I craved the gentleness in the air, the sun caressing my skin, relaxing tense muscles, erasing my worries.

I grabbed onto anything that anchored me solidly to the moment. My love for anything my senses had to offer: a melody, the colors of nature, a wonderful scent, all of it was home to me. And when my boyfriend held my hand, I felt protected, I felt his warmth in our hungry yet gentle intimacy; it anchored me into the present; it was the hand, the body, the soul that would catch me if I fell.

Later, I developed an enduring obsession for understanding, to help come to terms with the senselessness of the brutal experience of my birth. I remember the unexpected but fascinating clarity about how the world works, while realizing it is little wonder we repress the hopelessness and powerlessness of our struggle coming into this world. We will do anything not to remember our complete vulnerability in the face of our imminent destruction.

CHAPTER III

Family Bliss

I was left in my first foster home when I was nine months old.

In therapy, as I peeled off layers of my defenses, and forgotten events were revealed, I often wondered how I had survived the cruel world I had endured. Was it purely accidental? No. I discovered that despite the barbarism of my birth and its imprints that were compounded by layers upon layers of dreadful times in the years that followed, sweet memories of the first few months of life spent in the family home left just as much of an imprint. I found out that memories of gentleness and loving care were crucial to my survival and the key to my sanity.

*

My father is the person I remember most vividly. My mother is present but almost transparent, ghostlike in my memory of the earliest days.

My father's workshop was a paradise. It had white walls, wooden floors that smelled of wax, working tables and benches made of unfinished wood, leather hanging on the walls, leather on the tables, tools all over the place, and a large window opening onto a back street. I loved the smell of leather and wood mixed together, the sounds and rhythms of my father at work, the muffled noises coming from the other workshops in the alley down below, and every so often the crescendo of a circular saw screeching through wood. It was music to me, an enchanted world.

The best part was my father's presence. He always had a big smile on his face, and when he looked at me, there was tenderness in his beautiful blue eyes. He would scoop me up and show me around as if I had never been in his workshop before. He would explain things to me that I could not possibly understand, but I was quite happy to simply listen to the sound of his voice and the joy, the life in it.

At bath time, my mother would spread a bunch of towels on the dining table, set a metal washtub with large handles on them and pour warm water in until it was half full. She would shampoo my blond curls until the bubbly soap made me look "irresistible" to my father, the talented photographer. He would set up his camera to take pictures of his baby girl. Later in life, when I studied those photos, I admired the compelling and atmospheric quality of the black and white images he captured. It was a unique gift he had. In the darkroom, the images would slowly reveal themselves on the papers soaked with magic solutions.

It was my father who implanted the love of music in my heart.

In a treasured memory of mine, I am lying in my crib, surrounded by the peace and quiet that descended upon our home at bedtime. The world stopped moving, and all I could hear was a gentle whisper. The room was dark except for a small lamp in the corner that projected a soft glow behind my father, sitting next to me. I could see his silhouette hunched over his guitar against the orange glow. Then I heard the first notes, and soon the chords turned into tender songs, their pleasing rhythm rocking me ever so softly. The heavenly flow entered my ears, touched my heart, and seemed to diffuse itself like a musical mist throughout my body, reaching its every cell.

My eyes were wide open at first, but soon sleepiness took over, and after unconvincingly battling the blissful anesthesia, the dreams began. I could still hear the music that sang so far away, then it faded into silence.

This memory was buried for the longest time. Maybe it had been necessary to forget or impossible to reconnect to kindness, peace and beauty after the world had turned cold and ugly. Perhaps it was the only way to adjust to the new ways and to survive them.

But the memory was still there, alive inside me, even if not conscious. I kept hearing music in my head. I just did not know where it was coming from. But I know now that my father played for me night after night. Out in the big world, audiences would gather to hear him play. But at night, when he played, it was just for me, and he was mine, all mine.

As I started to uncover these forgotten early memories around my real father, they revealed the reason for my decade-long search for a classical guitar teacher - to recover that music and to reclaim the feelings of warmth, tenderness, safety, and joy. The world my father created for me was exciting, full of promise. There, I was alive without apology, doubt, fear, or shame.

I realized over time that when blocked memories too painful to bear disappear into our unconscious, entire sections of life disappear, and with them the beautiful, the kind, the gentle ones, as the brain does not discriminate. It feels as if years have fallen away, never to be recalled.

But consciousness restored both the unbearable and the sublime.

*

After a few months, the atmosphere in our home began to change. There were screams and there were tears. There were angry voices and fights, and it did not take long before Reine felt she had no choice but to divorce Louis.

Louis did not want the separation, but Reine had made up her mind, most likely under the influence of her relentless mother, who was finally getting what she had wanted all along. The divorce procedure started in 1952, but in the 1950s, getting a divorce was no small endeavor. Both my parents wanted custody, and a ferocious battle ensued that would end eight years later. Reine and Louis each had their own lawyers, whose job was to prove that the other parent was unfit to raise a child. During the unending battle, Reine and Louis kept pointing accusatory fingers at each other. It is not surprising that somewhere along the line my parents became enemies for life.

Louis could not take me with him until the court reached a decision. However, I remember that he sometimes showed up on the doorstep, and I always ran to him and jumped into his arms. On one such occasion, a very bitter fight started in the corridor between my parents. I was looking up at their faces; they were screaming at each other and suddenly, they each grabbed one of my arms pulling me in opposite directions like I was made of rubber. It scared me, and I began to cry. They stopped fighting but the hatred between them was tangible.

Hoping to someday open her own salon, Reine had started training at a famous esthetician's salon in Paris's wealthy "beaux quartiers." She was gone for long hours each day. I was told later in life that this was the reason I was sent to foster homes. My working mother did not have time to take care of me. This would have made sense if not for the fact that my grandparents lived right next door and my aunt Rose lived one flight of stairs above us with her family. With all these people around, why couldn't my mother come up with a better solution than foster care?

I always suspected that my grandmother had something to do with that decision and that my mother, overwhelmed by her failed marriage and a full-time job, followed in her mother's footsteps.

History was repeating itself.

EARLY LOSSES

I was nine months old when I was left in the care of Madame Pomaré. She was a gentle, caring woman; she loved me like I was her own. I bonded with this kindhearted soul. The mass of her white hair, her long black dresses, and more than anything, the tinkle of her laughter made me feel safe. She was my family. The house and the garden were fun places to explore; they were the home where I felt I belonged.

Just like my father, Madame Pomaré saved my life and sanity by imprinting memories of what unconditional love and acceptance looked and felt like. She enjoyed her life and the baby girl she had been entrusted with, she smiled often, laughed out loud, and let me be a carefree little child, giggling, playing, running, shouting, raging without reproach, anger, or worry.

We usually had lunch in the big, white tiled kitchen. She sat me down on the chair in front of an empty plate across from hers and I waited, happy to watch her move around the stove, singing while cooking steak. The delicious smell of melting butter and finely chopped garlic and the crackling sounds that came out of the pan as she carefully placed the steaks in it made my mouth water. She turned her head towards me with a gentle smile in her bluer-than-blue eyes, her skin pink from the heat. "Almost ready!" She exclaimed. Her joyful tone was contagious, my legs were moving as if running while trying to contain my impatience. And finally, the steaks landed on our plates. She approached with a sharp knife and a fork and began to cut mine into small pieces I could pick off the plate with my fingers. There were green beans there too, but the steak was far more interesting than the veggies. She poured us both a glass of water from an old chipped blue jug and finally sat down to eat. Seconds later, the front doorbell rang. "The postman!" She announced and quickly walked out of the kitchen. She opened the door and greeted the man she knew so well they were on a first-name basis. I finished my steak and patiently waited for her to return. The conversation was ongoing, and my patience wore off. I was still hungry, so I climbed and stood on the seat of my chair, reached out to her plate, and grabbed the good-looking steak getting cold from her plate. And I bit into the juicy, yummy thick slice and chewed it up until it was all gone. When Madame Pomaré came back, she took one look at her plate and burst out laughing. Her laughter still rings in my ears. It was loud, with a crystal quality to it, and above all, the most affectionate laugh I ever heard.

*

The day my father visited seemed blessed by the gods. I was very small, and I thought of the elements of my environment as friends. The trees in the garden sent their joyful signs. The rustle of their leaves was a language that I understood. The sun caressed me, and I felt its heat through the cotton of my white Sunday dress. It was a special day, not Sunday, but I wanted to put on my pretty dress for my father who was coming to visit. I wanted to dance, run, jump, and shout, to share my joy with my garden friends, the bees, and the ladybugs. The grass at my feet stretched out, soft as velvet, sprinkled with dewdrops, tempting me to lie down and roll in it.

"No," I said to the grass. "I can't get my pretty dress dirty."

The doorbell coughed softly. *Daddy is here!* My heart was beating wildly when he appeared at a bend in the path which ran by the house. He was big, blond, and smiling. I ran and threw myself into his arms. He lifted me, twirled, and twisted, causing peals of laughter.

After setting me back on the ground, he knelt before me. My little hands were still grasping his shoulders as he looked straight into my eyes. He was trying to read the intriguing mix of curiosity and sadness in them. It was a look that you can often see in the eyes of young children, a look that seems to penetrate all secrets, however deep or hidden. The expression on my father's face changed imperceptibly. He was looking for his words and having difficulty expressing himself.

"I've come to say goodbye. I must go far away for some time. I won't be able to come and see you on Sundays." He stopped for a moment. "But I'll come and fetch you as soon as I can. I promise you. Don't you ever, ever forget."

He took me in his arms, gave me a firm hug, deposited a kiss on my golden hair, then stood up and, without another word, turned around and walked away, as if he was in a hurry to depart, leaving me there with no time to say a word.

Time stood still. My throat tightened. In order not to disturb the absolute quiet inside, very softly, I whispered, "No." I sat and then lay down in the grass, looking at the sky that had turned several shades deeper. I immersed myself far and deep into its blue.

Even though my mother had instructed her not to let my father visit me, Madame Pomaré knew in her heart that I needed my dad as much as I did my mom. She felt that regardless of my parents' separation, depriving a child of her father was wrong. She also knew that Louis loved me, so she had disregarded the "agreement" and allowed the Sunday visits to continue secretly. Reine had never found out until that fateful day. When she heard of Louis' farewell visit, my mother became hysterical. She arrived on the doorstep late one morning, furious. She spoke fast and loudly, and what she said must have been terrible because Madame Pomaré's beautiful, gentle eyes filled with sadness. Teardrops rolled down her crinkled cheeks, burning forever into my heart the last image I would ever have of my beloved friend.

I remember the sound of heartbreak when her unwilling hand let go of mine.

CHAPTER IV

Onto Another Foster Home, Then Another ...

DARK, gray, dirty. A window with once white curtains, turned a dingy yellow. Pushed against the wall was a large bed with old, untidy sheets in which you could get lost, lost, lost. Nothing to curl up to. Nothing to look out upon. Silence. Cold. Loneliness. This is what Madame Dupré's house was like.

I remember a little boy with pink cheeks and a smile at the corners of his mouth, walking past my window once or twice. He was going somewhere. I was nowhere. That is all I remember.

One time, I tripped and fell face down onto the metal latch of the massive entry door. A gaping wound opened in my forehead between my eyes. Blood was pouring down my face. I was rushed to the hospital where the doctor called my mother. Until now, Madame Dupré had always had enough time before each of my mothers' occasional visits to clean up. This time, the place was shockingly dirty, especially my "room". There were loud words exchanged between the two women, words I did not understand but their tone was mean. Reine left and soon came back to take me away. Madame Dupré was very angry; she threw my unpacked clothes out the front door and onto the sidewalk before slamming the door shut. The scar on my forehead is still visible to this day.

*

Then, I was moved to a new foster home.

One day, my new foster mother, Madame Duval stomped toward me, brandishing a piece of white paper.

She was furious. She came close, towering over me. "Your mother!" she shouted, pointing at the paper fluttering in the wind. "She's taking you to another home; she'll leave you there! She doesn't love you anymore, you're bad, you'll be punished! Here, if you don't believe me, read it yourself!" she added, throwing the piece of paper at me, which flew away, turned around, and hugged a tree trunk behind her.

I did not know how to read, and I was too young to understand manipulation and lies. I believed her. In my universe, where my only lifeline was Reine and the hope that she would come and save me one day, the impact of Madame Duval's words was devastating.

I imagined dying.

The only way out – the end of the hurt.

It would just be like falling asleep.

"How can we die?" I asked a young boy who also lived at Madame Duval's. He looked puzzled for a moment; then, his face lit up as he replied, "If you eat candy wrappers, you'll die." I walked away in search of discarded wrappers, I found a few dropped on the ground, crumpled each one up into a little ball, and swallowed them one after the other.

At lunchtime, everyone gathered around the big wooden table outside. I remember that Madame Duval tried to force a spoon of mashed potatoes into my mouth, pushing hard against my lips, but my teeth were clenched tight. I just could not eat.

Furious, she ordered, "You will not leave this table until you swallow every last bit of the food on your plate!"

The other children left the table and began to play. I sat there as the afternoon crept away, my cheek on the table, eyes closed; it seemed to last forever. The sun went down, and darkness settled. Soon, I felt myself floating away from the plate of mashed potatoes, away from the table and the noises, above the trees, up to the dark, starry sky. I must have lost consciousness, adrift in a dream, delirious. When I opened my eyes, I saw Reine in tears. She was wrapping me in blankets. All I could think was, *I am in my mom's arms! I have been rescued!*

She put me in a car, nestled between her and the man at the wheel. We drove to a building that was all lit up. I was set down on a bed, which began to roll towards a room at the end of a corridor. The door swung open, then closed and the bed stopped moving.

The room was filled with bright lights, and there were lots of strange-looking people dressed in long white coats and hats.

31

They were bending over me with smiles I did not trust at all. It was then that I saw my mother's face, full of pain, looking in from the other side of the swinging doors. Why wasn't she in here with me? Why was she looking so sad?

Then, in a flash, I knew. This was the place Madame Duval had mentioned. The people in here were going to punish me. They were going to put me to sleep, and I would never wake up. I was going to disappear. I had not been rescued after all. So, I did the only thing I knew how: I fought with fists, and kicks and screams. But the doctors held me tight, still wearing their false smiles. I felt a sting in my arm and a funny feeling all over. *They're killing me, Maman! Don't let them!* So, I fought even harder. I felt another sting and then another, and finally, weakness overcame me. I was dying; I knew I was. It took several shots of anesthetic to counteract the waves of adrenaline rushing through my 4-year-old body.

The candy wrappers had caused a blockage that led to a burst appendix, an emergency that would have proved fatal if left unattended. Again, I experienced the pattern of chaos, fighting for my life, being overwhelmed, and then rescued.

I woke up, still far away but with a sense of being back. My eyes were still closed, and the curtains were drawn, but I knew it was daytime. The most indescribable joy came over me; I realized I was not dead. A sense of unreal happiness and serenity overtook me that usually accompanies the gift of life re-offered, another chance.

Slowly, my hand moved under the covers to reach the place that hurt a bit when I heard my grandmother's voice, concerned and kind. She put her hand over mine to prevent me from touching the freshly dressed wound.

I spent a few days there and made a friend, another little girl I shared a room with. Someone had brought me an expensive-looking doll, but the little girl had a cuddly, old, and ragged brown bear. We struck a deal; she kept my doll, and I walked out of the hospital with the bear, happy it was all mine.

CHAPTER V

The Red Bucket

ONLY A FEW WEEKS passed after my hospital stay before I was sent to Madame Valcourt's foster home.

It was just after lunch, and I had been allowed to go outside for a while. My new foster mother Madame Valcourt's backyard was alive. The sky was gray with patches of blue piercing the clouds here and there. The wind was blowing over the blades of the tall grasses. The trees looked like they were having a conversation in sign language as their branches moved wildly up and down, back and forth. I stood there watching the show, trying to decode what they were saying.

I was there for quite a long time, happily lost in the natural world when the need to pee brought me back, so I walked to the back door.

I tried to open it, but it would not move. I tried again, pushing against it slightly at first, then as hard as I could, but it still would not open. It was locked from the inside.

By then, I really needed to go, so I knocked, hoping someone would come. No one did. I sat down, trying to forget the sensation that was growing stronger. I just could not wait any longer. The pressure in my belly was too strong, so I ran to the tall grasses and pulled my panties down. I immediately felt better, got up, pulled my panties back up and looked down. Oh, no! I had hoped I was just going to pee, and no one would know, but I had done more than that. It was far from being invisible.

I left my spot and walked to the area behind the wall at the end of the house. There I discovered my small red bucket, lying on its side. It was one of those plastic toys that kids take to the beach to build sandcastles.

I picked it up and went back to cover the poop with the bucket upside down. From a distance, it was lost in the tall grass and only the top of the bucket could be seen. Almost perfect. I walked to the back of the garden and just sat there waiting for someone to unlock the back door. I brought my knees up to my chin, wrapped my arms around them, and waited. It was getting cold.

When I got too cold, I tried the door again, expecting resistance, but this time, it opened easily and walked inside, glad to feel the warm air. I went to my room and forgot about my little accident that had happened in the garden.

From the light outside, I knew the afternoon was drawing to an end. That was when I heard Madame Valcourt screaming in the living room.

"Taja, Emily, come here!" She sounded very angry.

Emily had only been there for a short while, and I had almost no contact with her. I was just four years old, and she was already twelve, so she went to school every day. She was a tall, shy-looking girl with straight brown hair, and she wore glasses when she was doing her homework. I am not even sure we had ever spoken.

Coming from opposite directions, Emily and I entered the living room at the exact same time, anxious about Madame Valcourt being so mad. She turned to me, then to Emily, and then back to me. Her eyes were mean.

"Which one of you pooped in the garden?" she screamed, swinging a whip with her arm. "Who was it?"

My stomach was in knots. I wanted to explain what had happened, but there was no time. Madame Valcourt was about to explode; she was not going to wait for a lengthy explanation. I could feel my hands turning cold, and my whole body was shaking. For a second, I felt I was going to throw up, but the sensation passed. Without thinking, and before I could stop myself, my hand pointed at Emily, and I heard myself say, "She did it."

In a flash, Madame Valcourt pushed me out of the room and slammed the door shut behind me. I heard a horrifying scream, so I ran to my room, and lay face down on my bed, covering my head with my pillow. After a while, I let go of the pillow and heard nothing. The house was as quiet as if no one lived there. I wondered about Emily, watched the flickering light on the outside porch, and fell asleep as night descended upon the house. I felt so sad, and so ashamed.

I woke up in the morning, later than usual. I had fallen asleep fully dressed. No one had come to get me, so I peeked outside and saw the bathroom door was open. The door to the living room was still closed, so I ran to the bathroom, then went back to my room. I sat on the edge of my bed, unsure of what to do next. I had not eaten the night before, and pangs of hunger were tugging at my stomach.

I got up and opened the door slowly and quietly. I could not see anyone, so I walked to the kitchen. Madame Valcourt was not there, but two people I had never seen before were sitting at the table, a man and a woman, who looked nice in their beautiful clothes. They looked surprised to see me. They both looked worried, the woman particularly. She must have been crying and still held a handkerchief in her gloved hand.

She smiled at me. "Hi, little girl," she said. "I'm Emily's mother. What is your name?"

"Taja," I replied, slightly intimidated.

"Taja, that's a pretty name."

Her voice was soft. She looked so sad, and her eyes were red and swollen.

"Taja, do you know where Emily is?" she asked.

I must have looked puzzled because she continued:

"My little girl ran away; we're looking for her everywhere. Did she tell you where she was going? Do you know why she ran away?"

At that moment, two men in funny costumes and hats walked in. I was told they were policemen looking for the missing child. They said something that seemed to ease the worry on Emily's mom's face. One of them looked at me as if he was going to speak, then changed his mind, turned around and walked out of the room accompanied by his colleague, and Emily's dad.

I never saw Emily again. I was told that she went back home to live with her parents. I felt happy for her and relieved that she had escaped. I wished I had escaped with her. And I hoped she had forgiven me.

I never found out if my mother ever learned of the incident. I often wondered why the police did not suspect that we were mistreated and why my mother had not come to take me home too.

CHAPTER VI

The Leaf

I WENT TO PRESCHOOL a few times a week; it was a Catholic school run by nuns. Before class started in the mornings, the kids would get up from their chairs and together say prayers aloud. I did not understand the reason for this strange behavior or the words that were recited, but I did know that I had to do the same. I watched one of the kids intently, moved my lips so that it would match the way his lips were moving, and I mumbled monotonous sounds so it would appear as if I knew the words. I was far too afraid and embarrassed to ask the teacher about this ritual.

Back from school, I was allowed to play in the garden but most days, I would stay in the house.

On the day Madame Valcourt had punched my nose, triumphantly exclaiming to one of her cronies, "this one is a bleeder!", I had escaped into the garden and just lay there until the sky turned dark, not moving, playing dead. Enveloped by the black of the night, I did not feel scared anymore. I hoped that they would forget all about me and that I could stay there just like that forever and ever.

I must have fallen asleep. When I heard a noise, I opened my eyes. A silhouette was standing over me. Too exhausted to move, I squinted and tried to distinguish the details of the shape in the dark. Then I heard Monsieur Valcourt's soft voice.

"Come on, girl, let's go inside. You're going to catch your death out here."

He leaned over and scooped me up. I put my arms around his neck as he started to walk towards the house. He took me to the bathroom, grabbed a towel from the rack, ran the water and cleaned the blood off my face.

He helped me wash my hands with soapy water, change my dirty clothes for a fresh pair of pajamas, and climb into bed.

"Are you hungry?" he asked. I shook my head a little.

He sat there with me, holding my hand. From time to time, he leaned over and caressed my curls and my cheek. I was not looking at him; my eyes were shut. I was just letting myself feel the healing gentleness of his touch. I fell asleep holding his hand.

The next day I was allowed to play in the garden. I sat by the door for a little while, just absorbing the quiet peace around me. It was springtime; wildflowers were growing all over now, patching the ground with colorful touches. There were dabs of blue in the sky, with big white cotton clouds passing in front of the sun every so often, changing the feel of the day, deepening the colors by a few shades. I spent some time observing the ever-changing shape of the puffy clouds; I could see jovial faces in them and some scary ones too.

In the left corner, away from the house, was a big chestnut tree boasting tender green leaves. Close to it, some unusual plants I had not noticed before were lined up by the side of the fence. I walked around them and finally sat down with my back against the solid and supportive tree trunk. There were blurry, distant images floating in my head of another place, another garden where there was beauty and solace. I still had a sense of it, but by now, too much time had gone by to remember. My heart was too swollen with sorrow. I had cried too many tears.

Suddenly, something on the ground caught my eye. It was a fallen leaf, abandoned, oblong, leathery-looking, and thick. It was of various shades of green and brown; it looked like the burl on a freshly cut piece of wood. I knew I had discovered something very precious, and it was just mine.

With great care so I would not risk damaging the find, I picked it up, then, using a corner of my button-down shirt, I began to clean it. It was shiny underneath the dust; I polished it some more until I ended up with a bright and resplendent jewel I promised myself I would cherish, always.

CHAPTER VII

Kicks & Screams

AS I WOKE UP, I felt tension and pain in my tummy. Madame Valcourt had instructed me not to leave my room in the mornings under any circumstances before she came in. Although I needed to go pee, I knew that Madame Valcourt would be furious if I went to the bathroom, which was just a few steps away. I tried to ignore the urge, but it would not go away. To make the sensation less intense, I lay down, pulled the covers over my head, curled up, and pressed my hands against my pajama pants between my legs; I hoped that if I pressed hard enough, the urgency would ease up. But it didn't.

I started shaking, and once again, just like most mornings since I had arrived, I felt my muscles relax down there. I was getting soaked. The pain in my tummy was over, but at the same time, I was possessed by an unspeakable terror. I knew what was going to happen next. I quickly ran to the radiator, warm at all hours of the day in the cold season. I climbed up and sat on it with the foolish hope that I might have just enough time to get dry, and then Madame Valcourt would not find out. It was silly because my sheets were wet too, but I needed to do something, anything. I could not bear to just lie there, waiting.

Some time went by, and I felt pleasantly anesthetized. But then I heard Madame Valcourt's heavy footsteps coming toward my room, getting closer, so I jumped down from the top of the radiator and quickly went back to my bed, pulling the covers up to my nose. The door swung open, and the large, red-faced woman entered.

"So, what do we have here?" she asked, her voice loud, a sardonic grin on her face.

She grabbed the blankets I was holding tight and brusquely yanked them away from the bed, sending them flying into the air, twisting and curling as they fell onto the floor.

"You did it again!" she screamed. "You! Filthy girl! I am going to teach you a lesson!" She stormed out of the room, and seconds later, she called. "Taja, come here! Right now!"

I quickly hid behind my bed.

"You better not keep me waiting, or I will come and get you!" she screamed again.

There was nowhere to escape, no one to beg for help. I came out of my hiding spot and walked across the corridor to the living room where Madame Valcourt was waiting for me with a whip in her hand. She snapped it in the air a few times, enjoying the terror in my eyes and the hunching of my body as I braced myself against the blows to come. I already knew all too well that the leathery whip cut like a knife into the flesh. Usually, the terror and pain were so unbearable that I could not help crying and begging despite the humiliation.

Suddenly, a long-contained rage exploded in me. Possessed, I ran at her, my eyes level with her fat bare knees, now only inches away. With all the strength I could muster, I started pounding on them with my fists as hard and fast as I could. The rumbling rush of adrenaline was so loud that the sounds faded away, the fear evaporated, and all that was left was an irresistible drive to fight. I threw myself at Madame Valcourt as the only option I had left, even if life itself was about to be lost. There was no chance of rescue. No arms to wrap themselves around me, protect the little girl, promise she will be okay, that she is not alone, that this will never happen again, ever, ever, ever.

The multi-tongued whip cut through the air, biting, and burning my skin. First it hurt! But then it didn't. I stopped feeling pain or just did not care anymore. I was David, she, Goliath. This time, Goliath was winning hands down. I felt hard kicks in my stomach. She had given up the whip, using her boots as a weapon. I felt a stabbing pain in my back. Bent over, I couldn't catch my breath, couldn't get air in my lungs. *I can't breathe… it's over. It's over now!* Before I slipped into unconsciousness, I thought, *it's so sad that I will never see my mom again.*

~ REFLECTIONS & INSIGHTS ~

I was a trainee at The Primal Training Center. Kyle, my boyfriend at the time, had slept at my place.

I woke up that morning and smiled; I felt light, a sense of wellbeing, a musical harmony, a calm happiness within myself, as the filtered sunlight streaming into the room announced the promise of another beautiful California day.

I opened my eyes and stretched out with a quiet yawn. The mattress lay on the light taupe carpeted floor. My right arm dropped to the floor, my hand touching the soft pile. Lazily, I turned away from him, taking in the view of the empty room. I looked across the floor and caught sight of Kyle's working boots. My eyes focused on the thick dirty rubber of their soles. An uneasy feeling came over me.

It was not the first time I had asked him to leave his boots outside the room. He hadn't listened. I felt something like a vague discomfort in the pit of my stomach. I shook it off, got up, and headed for the kitchen where I brewed coffee. The delightful scent in my cup caressed my nostrils. I took a shower, got dressed, and left, quietly closing the door behind me, on my way to the center for a session.

I found my old blue convertible Mustang parked down the street. I loved to ride down Olympic Boulevard, top-down, the sun warm on my face. Exhilarating. Paris crossed my mind; its capricious weather, busy streets, and cold dark clouds, their bellies full of rain, about to burst anytime.

In the distance, the ocean shimmered. *I'm living in paradise,* I thought. Excited, I accelerated, enjoying the speed, the wind like a giant blow-dryer making my hair float away and back, tickling my cheeks. I wished I could go faster. The Eagles' song "Heartache Tonight" came on the radio. The music was in perfect harmony with my elated mood.

I arrived at the Primal Training Center, happy to meet Jonty, who welcomed me with a heartfelt smile. We went straight to the soundproof padded room and dimmed the light. I lay down on the foam-covered floor while he settled quietly behind me.

I wondered if I needed a session at all. My mind was full of sunshine. Nothing troubling was nibbling at my subconscious door. I said as much to Jonty. "Nothing much to report today; I feel good."

Silence behind me.

I found it difficult to lie there, quiet, and motionless. I needed to move. I got up and started walking back and forth, ending up facing the foam-covered wall that I unexpectedly punched slightly, without much conviction, but something disquieting was on the rise, it was not so pleasant anymore.

"I'm feeling good," I insisted, unconvincingly.

Jonty picked up on it. "Really?" he asked.

His question irritated me. I pounded the wall again, meaning it this time. My good mood was crumbling like a kicked sandcastle.

"What's happening?" Jonty's voice echoed my thoughts.

"Dunno," I said. Suddenly, I slid down the wall like a rag doll and sat, looking down at my legs, empty-minded, deflated, defeated.

"What was that punch about?" Jonty's voice came out of a dark corner.

I did not know, but his questions felt more and more irritating. "I *was* feeling good, and now it's all gone!" I said reproachfully.

"You sound upset," he replied calmly, matter of fact.

"I am." I thought about it. "I'm... upset..." The words came out, feelingless. I hesitated. Then a small voice came out, "Your questions, they upset me... "

"Really?" Jonty asked, encouraging.

I just sat there. *"I'm such a coward,"* I thought. I felt overwhelmed. "I'm a coward." I said it out loud this time.

"What do you mean?" Jonty asked.

"I'm afraid to get angry ... at *you*!"

"What will happen if you do?"

"You'll be mad at me. You will hate me!" I replied, emphasizing the word "hate."

"Hate you?" His voice was curious, disbelieving.

I turned my head and looked at him. His eyes were kind. No hate there.

I got up again, facing away, the blank blue wall right in front of me. I was so tired, yet something inside made me want to punch. I tried again, barely making a dent in the foam.

"Say the words," Jonty insisted.

I knew I had to, so I did. "I'm angry." The words sounded flat, empty, meaningless. I felt stupid.

Jonty's voice behind me was powerful. "Again!" he said.

"I'm angry." For a few seconds, I felt I was floating away. My words, my voice, my punches, disconnected from each other.

"Again!"

So, I pounded the wall repeatedly and then added the words of anger.

For a short while, there was still a disconnect between the punches and the words, but then they became one. I began to scream and pound in concert.

"It was a beautiful day, and you took it away! Why did you do that? How could you? You took it away!"

I was still in the present, yelling at Jonty for ruining my beautiful day, but something else was on the rise. It felt like rage and terror wrapped together, inseparable. I was pounding, pushing, raging at that wall. Suddenly, I saw boots flashing in front of me. Boots! Kyle's boots on the floor this morning!

I screamed at him. "Why can't you keep your damn boots out of my room?! I hate them; I hate them, I hate *you*!" I was shaking with rage, just pure red-hot rage. His boots on the floor, their thick dirty rubber soles, they felt dangerous, brutal, so very brutal.

Suddenly, I felt a stab in my stomach.

The pain brought tears to my eyes, but the hurt intensified, spreading to my back and down to my legs. I began to shake with that strange mix of fear and rage.

I descended into the devastated sobbing of a young child as flashes of memories were coming to mind in bits and pieces that made no sense. Madame Valcourt's ugly face of rage and hatred. The whoosh of a whip cutting through the air, a scream, Kyle's boots, my room back there, a radiator.

This is it! I'm losing it!

I fell on my knees while pounding the wall like never before. I was beside myself. Tears and screams, an endless supply, my heart beating so fast, shaking, in terror, but no words. And just as I realized it was life or death, I finally saw before me that day.

I was stunned. I had been dancing around that memory for a long time. The adult was walking along with the little girl during the terrifying reawakening of times spent at Madame Valcourt's, looking at that face of rage and hatred in the eye.

That scene had left an imprint of its own. It had been buried deeper, beneath my birth imprint, even less accessible, a second-line experience with first-line valence. It matched my birth imprint: the impossibility of staying put, the necessity of fighting my way forward, without help and all alone.

I also realized that the depth of the trauma is much more profound when the pain is inflicted with deliberate cruelty. No matter how abusive an adult is, to survive, the child will always feel at fault. There is hope in being responsible because it protects him from the unbearable reality of being hated and gives him a sense of being in control. If it was my fault, then if I changed, if I was good enough, maybe …

CHAPTER VIII

The Visit

I REMEMBER waking up one day to a feverish atmosphere in the house. Monsieur Valcourt was out of sight and had been for a few days. A couple of ladies I had never seen before came over and spent the day cleaning the house with Madame Valcourt. They removed the sheets and made the beds with fresh ones, swept the floors, dusted, and waxed the furniture. Later, wonderful smells of apple pie floated in the air. I did not understand what all this effervescence was about, but I welcomed it because it had brought new people to the house, and it felt safer that way. As long as Madame Valcourt was busy, she would not pay attention to me.

There were moments that day when she would look at me, with a puzzled look on her face. She smiled now and then, but it did not look like a smile, more like a grimace, and I did not know what to make of it.

The following day, one of the two ladies came back. She came into my room that morning with breakfast and a smile. She stayed with me while I ate and told me about a visit I had to be prepared for. She ran a bath and washed me all over while I was soaking in the soapy water, then she rinsed my hair until the water was clear. When I stepped out of the bath, she dried me with a clean, thick towel. When she tried to dry between my legs, I jumped back and pushed her away. She looked puzzled but handed me the towel and let me dry myself, then took me back to my room and began to brush my hair while it was still damp.

She opened the armoire. There was a pretty white dress on a hanger. I had never seen it before.

She gave me clean panties, white socks with a lace border, a white sleeveless shirt to keep me warm, and then, helped me slip into the beautiful white dress with embroidered flowers on it. She played with my curls until she was satisfied with the way they looked and finally gave me a pair of white shoes with laces that she tied perfectly. She then inspected the result of her work and smiled, looking quite pleased with herself.

That is when I heard the doorbell ring. The expected visitors had arrived.

First, I heard the front gate opening, its rusty hinges screeching. Then came the sound of shoes walking up the alley to the front door and several polite voices. The visitors were led into the living room where I had been told to sit and wait. Suddenly, my mother appeared before my eyes. For one split second, I thought I was dreaming, but the next second, unable to restrain myself, I ran towards her and jumped into her arms. She was very real, and my nose was planted in her beautiful mass of red hair and its wonderful smell. She laughed and tried to push me back so she could look at me, but I would not let go of her. I was clinging on to her like the survivor of a shipwreck hangs on to a lifebuoy.

A man accompanied my mother. She called him Damien. He was very reserved. He smiled politely, but I could tell that he did not like it here. Maybe he did not like Madame Valcourt.

Both were invited to sit down. The lady who had helped me get dressed kept coming out of the kitchen to serve coffee and cake. I did not know what the conversation was about, I did not care for cake or anything I was offered. I had brought a chair right next to my mother's, and I was holding on to her skirt. All I wanted was to be near her.

Someone asked me to go to the center of the room. Madame Valcourt lifted me onto a wood chair to show me off. The moment she grabbed me, I felt separated, dissociated. Everything and everyone in the room began to feel distant and unreal. Then, she asked me to turn around for my mother to see how pretty I was in my white dress, and I followed orders, turning around like a little doll a few times, then stopping, facing Reine.

Madame Valcourt's face lit up, and there was a proud smile on it. I was mesmerized by her duplicity. Her lips were lifted on each side of her mouth, giving it the shape of a smile, but above her mouth, nothing was moving. Her nose and her eyes did not wrinkle out of shape. Did she really imagine that Reine would not see the evil woman that she really was?

I was waiting for my mother to get up and scream at Madame Valcourt. But she didn't. It did not matter because she was going to take me away from here anyhow. I wondered why Reine and the man she called Damien stayed as long as they did because all I wanted was for us to leave.

When my mother and Damien got up, I got up too.

" Wait!" I ran to my room, fetched my leaf, grabbed a sweater, and ran back to them ready to go.

My mother knelt down and explained,

"We have to go now, but you are staying here, my darling." She kissed the top of my head and gave me a hug. Then she pushed me back to take a good look at me, and there were tears in her eyes.

I screamed, "No, no, Maman, Maman, please don't leave me here, oh no, don't go, don't, don't, please don't!" I was out of breath, hysterical, but I could not stop begging and crying. As she stood up, I grabbed her jacket, then I hung onto her leg with all my might, my feet lifted off the ground so the weight of my four-year-old body would make it impossible for her to walk away. I would not let go. I was shaking with rage and despair.

Someone grabbed my hand and forced it open, one finger at a time, and I felt my body being torn away from my mother's."

I was screaming without any restraint. But one second, my mother was here, the next she was gone, and Damien with her.

I heard the front gate open and close. Then I was set free, so I ran to the front door, turned the knob, slammed it open and made it to the gate. A narrow ledge ran along the bottom. I stepped on it while holding on to the black metal spears pointed toward the sky and pulled myself up enough to get an unobstructed view of the road.

They were walking inexorably toward the car parked down the road, and there was nothing I could do, but I kept begging, screaming and sobbing like nothing was ever going to stop me. They did not turn around. The most striking memory I have of that moment is my mother's long dark red hair floating on her back as she was walking further and further away. Away from me.

Again, I remember like it was yesterday, the sounds and the feel of heartbreak. No word can convey the nightmarish emotions of a time like this. Today, I am certain that this was the moment when our already strained mother-daughter bond broke. I had to give her up just like she had given me up.

But she never knew.

*

Not long after my mother's visit, Madame Valcourt decided to leave the city and spend the summer months in a country house in southern France.

I still remember the old, isolated farmhouse, a couple of mysterious crumbling sheds further away, plenty of open space around the house and beyond it, fields of wheat extending as far as the eye could see. I spent most days by myself walking, first around the house, then further and further away, bathing in a peaceful silence, away from slamming doors and angry voices. Being alone felt wonderfully safe; the open space offered a possible escape anytime, although the vastness of this new summer domain was a bit intimidating.

Sometimes there was not even a touch of wind, and the whole world was immobile and quiet, but often a slight breeze whispered reassuringly. As the ripe wheat grasses gently moved in the wind, their seedheads bending, shifting directions, the color of the fields would change to a deeper blond. I wanted to jump and run around in the inviting, friendly grasses. But I just stood there, watching, anesthetized by the heat of those sunny days.

A small meandering road was bordered on each side by a ditch full of green grasses and curly dried-up leaves. By the edge of the ditches, there were bushes with raspberries and blackberries. On a sweltering afternoon, as I was leaning over to pick a juicy-looking red berry, one foot planted on each side of the ditch, I heard a slight noise below me. I looked down. A strange-looking animal was slithering with ease, but it had no legs that I could see. Its back was a dark gray color, with a pattern of black geometrical shapes all over it. I froze, held my breath, a bit frightened because I had never seen anything like it before, but at the same time, I was moved by its presence. I was not alone; I had found a friend. It slid away quickly, and I resumed picking berries.

The weather that summer reached record high temperatures, and I was thirsty all the time. Madame Valcourt would give me only half a glass of cold tea each day. That's all she would let me drink. In hindsight, I can only imagine that it was her way to ensure I wouldn't wet my bed.

At first, it was just the feeling of my lips being too dry, and I would lick them all day long. My mouth felt like cardboard, even more so at night when I would wake up feeling weak all over. I often became dizzy, but I could not tell anyone. I knew that Madame Valcourt would only explode with evil laughter at any complaints from me or would find a new twisted way to punish me.

On a quiet afternoon, I walked by the downstairs toilet next to the back door. Curious, I entered the small room and looked down at the water in the toilet bowl. Staring me in the face was the solution to my problem. Of course, I was too young to understand the risks of drinking unsanitary water. But I did realize I had to be extremely careful not to be caught. Otherwise, I would be forbidden to drink and punished for it. I could not risk losing access to my newly discovered water supply.

Most afternoons, when I was sure that everyone had gone to sleep for an after-meal siesta, I entered the small closet, knelt down by the toilet bowl, and cupping my hands to retain the water, I drank and drank and drank until I was full. Water had never tasted so good.

~ REFLECTIONS & INSIGHTS ~

It was 1978, and my three-week intensive therapy was beginning the following morning. I had checked into a hotel located on a boulevard around the corner from Almont Drive, within short walking distance from the Primal Institute. I settled into a nondescript room where I would spend time alone, away from distractions such as radio, television, and away from interactions with friends and family.

After a day in the sun and swimming in the ocean, I was quite tired. I lay down for a while wondering what tomorrow would bring, feeling a mix of excitement and slight anxiety of the unknown. I set the deafening alarm clock I had brought with me and, soon after, fell asleep.

It was 4 a.m. when I woke up with a violent burning sensation in my bladder. I knew it too well. These infections had been plaguing me for many years. Back in Paris, my doctor regularly prescribed a course of antibiotics that brought me quick relief from the pain.

As I reached for my bag, I remembered that I had not packed my medication as specific instructions were given not to take any drugs during the intensive therapy. I waited, feeling cold, shaking, arms wrapped around my tummy, scared that I wouldn't be able to handle the pain until the start of my morning session.

The next day, I entered the Primal Institute's dark reception room. A few minutes later, a door opened, and Gretchen, my three-week therapist, welcomed me with a smile and showed me to a small, padded room with low lights and tissue boxes scattered around. As I lay down on the mattress, she sat on the floor behind me.

"How are you feeling?" she asked.

"I have a bladder infection, and it hurts. It started in the middle of the night, but I did not have my medication, and I did not know what to do!"

Gretchen inquired about the infection, the pain level, the recurrence, who treated me and how. She also reassured me that it would not be a problem if I took antibiotics.

I felt the tension in my body ease up a bit. Gretchen asked if I had noticed any particular times when these infections happened. I did not know why, but Michael came to mind, so I told her about him.

I had met this tall Canadian guy whose swagger reminded me of Mick Jagger. He lived in the house where I was a temporary guest when I first arrived. I was attracted to him with his curly brown hair and warm eyes. I watched him from afar while I was lying by the pool, the sun darkening my skin, enjoying the quiet, barely disturbed by the distant city noise below us. Michael invited me to visit his small garden by the side of the house where he grew appetizing looking tomatoes and aromatic herbs. As we walked along the sandy path, he asked if I would have dinner with him that evening. I nodded, too shy and intimidated to show my enthusiasm. From that moment on, we spent days and nights together until yesterday, when he had dropped me off at the hotel.

I was quiet for a while, not sure what to do, what to say. My mind wandered, but Michael's face came back into focus, and tears welled up. I wiped them away. The quiet room and the dimmed lights felt comforting.

Gretchen whispered, "Something made you cry." It was not a question but invited a response.

"Looking at Michael ..." Sadness was building up inside me; I was trying so hard to hold back the tears.

A compassionate murmur broke the silence, and I felt my throat closing up; words did not want to come out. Grief insinuated itself inside of me, deepening, almost too thick to bear. I was holding my breath until I couldn't.

"I don't want to lose him!" I blurted out. The thought of losing him ...! *Oh! No, I couldn't lose him. What if he left me?* My chest was going to explode; salty water was burning my eyes.

"Tell him ..." she said, her voice quietly inviting me to go on.

Her words unlocked a door somewhere; the sadness couldn't hide away. I started to cry deeper this time, longer, relieved by her words and the kind tone in her voice.

I whispered, "If he left me ..." I heard my voice break.

"If he left you?" It was not a question, more like a kind, sad voice echoing my own.

"Oh no, he can't, he can't!"

"Ask him not to." Her voice was firmer now. Once again, I felt I was treading on dangerous ground and, I wanted to retreat to ... *where?*

Finally, I whispered, "I don't want you to leave me Michael."

"Please ..." she encouraged me with that one word.

Timidly, in a low voice, almost ashamed, I said, "I don't want you to leave me. Please don't, please..." My chest was heavy with pain, too many tears trapped inside, my throat too tight to let them flow out.

Gretchen said, "Please, Michael..."

I had to say *that*! If I didn't, my chest was going to explode. "Don't leave me, Michael, please ... don't ..." and that was when the dam broke. "Please don't leave me, please, please don't!" I was crying buckets of tears, my entire being in that moment, in that feeling.

Michaels' face faded, and another moment back in time took its place. The words now, almost a scream: *"Maman! Maman! Maman!"* I curled up, as powerful sobs flowed out of me; I was the inconsolable 4-year-old girl again. Above the sounds, deep into the tears, I heard a voice coming out of me, that of a little girl who was watching her mother walk away, leaving her behind with Madame Valcourt in that awful foster home.

I remembered hanging on to her leg with all my weight to make it impossible for her to walk, and not letting go. I remembered shaking with fear, rage, and despair, then my body torn away from my mother's. Once again, I ran and screamed for her; I knew she could hear me. I ran to the gate, climbed that ledge, grabbed the bars and lifted myself so as not to lose sight of her. And once again, I watched in disbelief as she walked away. *She was really leaving me there. Yes, she was …*

That image had been in my mind for years, and I often wished I could have painted it but did not know why or how. That specific memory was only visual. Until now, I had never remembered the powerful emotions attached to it, beneath the repression.

The abandoned child kept on crying, calling *Maman*, until there were no more tears, and the room became quiet again. I had cried a river of tears, crumpled up tissues littered the floor. I lay there for a while, letting myself come back to the present, bathing in an unusual sense of calm.

I was shocked by how moments separated by decades had come together, connected by the same feeling, like beads on a string: *Please don't go, don't abandon me*, the same pain from Michael to my mother, dreading, anticipating abandonment.

The pain in my bladder was gone! And that was when I realized that I hardly ever drank. I had spent years forgetting to drink. Drinking was associated with the pain of abandonment deep in my unconscious. In order not to feel that pain, I acted out by keeping myself dehydrated, and I had become desensitized to the sensation of thirst.

From that moment on, I had a way out, now conscious of my need to drink, slowly realizing to what extent I had deprived myself, that the lack of fluid intake must have triggered the many physical infections. I was able to reeducate myself, and step by step, I began to experience the almost-forgotten sensation of thirst. From then on, bladder infections became a thing of the past.

CHAPTER IX

Monsieur Valcourt's Secret

LATER in life, as the story unfolded, I remembered that I was glad when Monsieur Valcourt was around. Compared to his massive wife, he was a small, pale man. He had very little say in the affairs of daily life. He would come and go, and sometimes he would disappear for days at a time.

Monsieur Valcourt had his own room in the back. It looked completely different from the rest of the house. A colorful rug covered the floor with dancing twirls all over it. Old pictures were hanging on the dirty white walls. A small bed on the left was pushed to the side, a lamp on a stand next to it, a desk stood in the middle of the room, a light on top of it, and an oversized armchair faced the door. Each time

I had been in this room, the curtains had been drawn, and both lamps were on, fighting the dark, but doing a poor job of it. A few toys littered the floor. I was not allowed to take them out of the room, so I would sit on the floor, pick up a bear, and let myself feel what it was like to hold something soft and fuzzy.

Monsieur Valcourt was sitting in the big armchair and softly called my name. "Come here, come sit on my knee," he said with a look on his face I did not recognize.

I liked him, and I was not afraid of him. He was an ally, and although he was not there very often, he was always kind to me. However, I hesitated.

"Come on, Taja," he said with an urge in his voice. Still holding the bear in one hand, I took a few steps forward until I was close enough for him to grab me and pull me onto his lap. He had a funny smile; his eyes were dark and teary. He began caressing my hair.

"You have such pretty hair," he complimented, still caressing me with his long white fingers. I had never taken notice of his fingers before, but now I was fascinated by them, I could not get my eyes off them as they were moving down from my cheek to my blouse that he unbuttoned slowly. He touched my chest for a moment, and then I felt his cold hand sliding down to my belly, feverishly feeling its way into my panties. It finally came to rest between my legs.

When he started caressing me there, I froze. I did not make a sound. He kept moving his fingers between my legs, and I began to feel very strange and wet down there. My chest felt tight, I could not breathe, I felt hot and sweaty, I dropped the bear. I wanted to run, but I couldn't.

I felt something growing below my buttocks as if a little animal was moving there. It was becoming hard, and Monsieur Valcourt loosened his belt with his other hand, reached into his pants, and touched himself there. His hand moved under my buttocks, and he was breathing harder and faster. Staring at the grimace on his face, I thought he was in pain. He did that for a while, at times caressing me. Then he opened his mouth and let out a weird noise followed by a big sigh.

After a minute or so, he looked at me and said, "This must be our secret. You know that don't you?" I quickly nodded in approval.

He got me dressed, and with a gentle slap on the back, he sent me away.

When we were left alone in the house, he would take me in there and turn the key in the lock so we would not be disturbed. Sometimes he was in such a rush that he forgot to lock the door; he grew bolder and more careless as time went by.

One terrible day, Madame Valcourt came home unexpectedly, called out for her husband, and, not waiting for an answer, opened the door he had forgotten to lock again. She took in the scene for a couple of seconds, gasped, backed out of the room, and slammed the door shut.

I was so scared; I never wanted to leave that room. I knew I had done something wrong.

Monsieur Valcourt looked crushed, shrunken. Madame Valcourt was the very embodiment of fury. She ordered him out, violence raging in her voice. He walked to the door and stepped into the corridor. I followed him closely, using him as a human shield.

Madame Valcourt began to yell just as her husband stepped out; curses were pouring out of her mouth like overflowing sewer water. She used words I had never heard before; they were just sounds to me, but her tone spoke volumes. He stayed quiet, and his silence enraged her even more. She approached him, pushed him, then tried to hit him, but he took a step back to dodge the blow. Missing the target, she lost her balance and collapsed onto the floor. This was when it got terrifying; she was just sitting there, her back against the wall, her fat legs apart, emitting wild teary cries that made my skin crawl. Then she burst into a hysterical laugh she had no control over.

The storm passed, and quiet returned. Madame Valcourt disappeared to another part of the house. Monsieur Valcourt sent me back to my room and retreated into his. This time, I heard him lock the door.

*

That night, I woke up lying on a hard surface, unable to move; I did not know where I was or how I got there. I was cold and terrified. *I must be dreaming. I must wake up. Now.*

The room was almost entirely dark, but a light bulb above my head gave just enough light to see the wooden surface I was lying on. *The kitchen table!* I tried to turn to my side but could not.

I focused my attention on the noises I could hear, heavy breathing, and a sound like the clinking of cutlery. I watched Madame Valcourt, her head turned to the side, looking down. I was naked, exposed, utterly vulnerable. I shivered. I wanted a blanket to hide and warm up under.

Fully awake now, words caught in my throat, *what am I doing here? I can't move. I'm scared.* Her silence was terrifying. I wanted to curl up in a little ball. I tried to but could not.

The house was perfectly quiet; not a sound came from the other rooms. *If I screamed, no one would come, would they?*

Then I heard the same noise again, right next to the table; the sound cutlery makes when setting the table.

It did not make any sense. Suddenly, I felt the rough touch of her hand on my thigh. She reached between my legs and kept her hand there. I felt something cold pushed inside me. A sudden and sharp pain made me scream. Terror broke loose as repeated throbs of unspeakable pain passed through my body like tidal waves.

Nothing was quiet anymore, millions of little beings inside of me had awakened, and they all screamed at once, in the racing of my heart, the quivering of my skin, in the way my throat tightened, and my muscles tensed, turning my body into a stone statue.

As Madame Valcourt stood over my body, I saw the face of pure evil. I remember closing my eyes and willing my mind to take me away, then, mercifully, I became so light that I lifted off the table, drifted to the ceiling and looked down. There I was on the table, my wrists tied together, stretched behind my head, my legs spread out and bound by something I could not see. The crazy woman's gray hair, her instruments of torture neatly laid out next to her. I saw my eyes were closed as if I was resting peacefully. There was no sensation left, no pain. I absorbed the details of the scene, the grain of the wooden table, the color and the shape of my curls spread out on it, the weave of the cloth the knives and forks were resting on, and how pale my body looked. And then, nothing.

I woke up in my bed. I felt nothing at first. Maybe it was that moment of transition between the state of sleep and awakening when the memory has not quite reached consciousness yet. But as I woke up, I screamed, curled up, and brought my hands to the fold between my thighs. I could not remember what had happened. I did not know why I was in my room at this late hour or how long I had been there. But I felt as if the vital energy necessary for life had all been used up. I was anesthetized, and just wanted to lie there and never move again, slip away somehow.

The shadows and the lights came and went. I slept. Sometimes, I detected muted light through the drawn curtains, other times, it was so dark I could have been floating in space. I did not mind. All was well. I was so tired.

Once in a while, I drank water from a glass left by my bedside. I thought about my leaf, my treasure.

Maybe a day or two, maybe more had passed before I felt the sleepiness dissipate. There was energy in my body I had not felt in a while, so I got up. Still wearing pajamas, I opened the door and listened. It was quiet, so I ventured out of my room and tiptoed in the direction of the kitchen.

Madame Valcourt appeared in the doorway. She asked me if I wanted something to eat. I nodded. She told me to go back to my room, and soon, she came in with a tray and put it on the side table.

"When you are done eating, get dressed and go outside to get some fresh air," she simply said before leaving.

On the tray, there was a plate with two slices of fresh bread with butter on them and a glass of water. I ate the tasty bread and drank the water, then went to my dresser, picked a pair of pants and a sweater, and changed. I went to the back door and looked outside. No one was there.

The clouds covered the sun every so often, and the air felt cold when they did. But then, the sun came out, and the air became warm. Sitting in the grass at the edge of the property, I let the warmth in; I absorbed it like a dried-out sponge absorbs water.

This was a good moment, almost a happy one. I lay down in the velvet grass, focused on each blade as if I was looking through a microscope. Then I looked up and spoke to the sun because it was my friend; when it shone so bright, I felt it was touching me with a healing wand, and I wept in its imaginary arms.

Until there were no more tears. My eyes were so swollen I could barely open them. Then I fell asleep in the sun's warm embrace with the scent of the grass in my nose.

I had lost sense of time when my mother came to fetch me. By then, I felt nothing, just removed, disconnected from the world around me.

I remember the rushed visit to the pediatrician after she found blood in my panties. I remember lying on a cold table, my panties being removed and the kind doctor looking somewhere between my legs. I felt myself floating again above and away from the table, my confusion and my nakedness were too much to bear.

~ REFLECTIONS & INSIGHTS ~

The evening group at the Primal Institute in Paris had just ended. We climbed back up to the ground floor, from the big group room below that we had left littered with banged-up tissue boxes. People were standing or sitting here and there, making plans to meet at a nearby café. I walked to the notice board by the office door. As I was inspecting the ads, a cut-out newspaper article caught my attention. I began to read the horrific account of what had happened to a young girl who had been violently sexually abused by two of her uncles. Suddenly, words were dancing on the paper, knife ... stuck ... vagina ... damage ... I stopped breathing. Ravaging pain was tearing at my vagina.

Galvanized by rage, I was propelled downstairs back to the big therapy room, now empty and dark. I screamed; I pounded like never before but felt no relief. I just couldn't break through into the memory and experience my distress in its true context. I collapsed onto the floor, out of breath, exhausted with a foreboding of dreadful things.

Since my three-week intensive therapy in Los Angeles, I had been free of panic attacks, but now they were back. Waves of terror ran through me, throwing me around without mercy. I was losing control of my life once more. Because of this, Art Janov sent me to a doctor for a prescription of Thorazine he used to gate trauma from infancy and to prevent overload which, in my case, was manifesting as panic attacks. The medication had a paradoxical effect and broke down my last defenses. I will never forget the day when walking down a familiar

Parisian street, suddenly, I hallucinated, the world upside down. The rooftops were on the ground, the lower levels touched the sky. It was a horror show.

I told Art. He thought I was not taking enough medication and recommended that I double the dose. What followed was complete disintegration. I later realized that I was re-living sensations of birth, triggered by the medication, but horribly out of context. I lost my grasp on reality and began cutting myself just deep enough to feel pain and see blood in a desperate attempt to stay connected to reality. As counterintuitive as it was, this self-destructive act was an attempt to protect myself from the terror I had of losing my sanity.

Mercifully, an uncle on my mother's side of the family, Raphael, realized that such a startling change in my behavior made no sense. He picked me up one afternoon and took me to consult a friend of his, a professor in psychiatry who ran the department at a reputable hospital. The professor asked me a few questions and the moment I mentioned Thorazine, he looked up from his notes and exclaimed, "Don't look any further, and stop it immediately." Thorazine was the culprit. After my uncle's timely intervention, it took just 48 hours off the medication for the terror to subside and for me to recover my sanity and my ability to function. Soon after my recovery, I opened a language school that quickly became successful. This restored my belief in myself. While I had been in a mental free fall, Reine and Damien had requested a meeting with Art who told them that I was "too damaged" to heal. To me, it was a condemnation I thought I would never recover from. But, devastated as I was, I had to fight, I had to, and prove to myself that Art's diagnosis was dead wrong! So I did.

While I was recovering from the agony of the Thorazine episode, the story in the article faded. But from time to time in the following years, I would feel a remnant of that tearing sensation in my vagina. I would remember the story in the article on the bulletin board, and my reaction to it, but it seemed distant and unreal.

When I first began to remember the night after Madame Valcourt found her husband masturbating while I was sitting on his lap, I discarded it as a false memory. But the recurrence of that sensation in my vagina each time I thought about the article pinned on the noticeboard at the Paris Institute told me that, regardless of my doubts, the memory of something awful was trying to enter my consciousness that night. However, it remained my deepest secret because I could not risk not being believed.

Over time, I realized why I had blocked any trace of the existence of a man living at Madame Valcourt's for decades. *By removing this essential piece of information, I blocked the entire sequence of events that followed.*

I understood two things after that. One was my lifelong distrust of women, and consequently the repulsion I felt as a teenager when my mother or my grandmother came near me or touched me. The other was my attraction to strong, sensitive men and how good life was in their company because then, I escaped both Monsieur Valcourt, the clandestine sexual abuser, Madame Valcourt, the vicious sexual abuser, and later, my stepfather Damien, the cruel emotional abuser.

The body always remembers. As I was reliving that scene with a friend and fellow trainee, I now understood why bruises appeared around my wrists that Madame Valcourt had tied down on that horrific night.

And that pain in my vagina as if something sharp was pushed against its wall, now made sense, triggered anytime I thought about that horrific article I read in Paris years earlier.

And it made sense that penetration hurt when there was little emotional intimacy, reminding my body if not my mind of that night long ago. My skin would feel the same cold, the present moment turned unreal as I dissociated from myself, from the man, from the moment as I had back then. I was ashamed of admitting the pain when making love, afraid it would make me "not good enough" for love, that I would be mocked, rejected, or abandoned. So, when it hurt, I made believe it was pleasure.

Monsieur Valcourt's molestation had forever locked together sex and affection in my psyche, so I craved touch and tenderness; I knew how it felt even if I did not know why. I slept around searching for it. But there never was enough touch, there never was enough warmth, enough reassurance. Nothing was ever enough.

CHAPTER X

New Home, New Rules

I WAS SHY of six years old when I returned from a life in foster homes, and started living with Reine and Damien, the man who was to become my stepfather.

Damien was the youngest son in a family of six. His siblings were much older, only his sister Lina was close to him in age. A couple of years after Lina was born, their mother, Katia, gave birth to a boy who died very young. His name was Damien. Perhaps to dampen her sorrow, she became pregnant again, and nine months later gave birth to a healthy baby boy that she named Damien in memory of the baby she had lost.

I suspect that Katia's fear of losing the newborn Damien set the stage for the way he was going to be raised by four older sisters and a mother who made a fuss about the new baby. Growing up, there seemed to be no rules to rein him in, nor boundaries he was forbidden to cross. Even his most unreasonable requests were always met with approval. When he wished to drink out of a crystal glass, he was given his own crystal glass; if he wanted to eat his food with silver cutlery, his mother would run to get it. His wish was their command. He told me that he was once sent to summer camp, and he did not like it there, so he wrote a letter to his parents saying that he had been bitten by a snake. Once they got there, they found out he had lied, but they just laughed about it and brought him back home. He loved to tell this story, maybe because it showed that he was in control of everyone around him.

The Bivas family was Jewish; during the war they had to flee and hide. But Damien, then a young adult, was sent to Portugal to stay with family. He was safe there and had a wonderful time, spending his days at the beach. He was popular with the girls: he was good-looking with his dark curly hair, bright blue eyes, and healthy skin that tanned easily. The days he spent in Portugal as war was raging in Europe were some of the happiest days of his life. He loved the country and learned to speak Portuguese. In our home, the only music he ever listened to in the early days were songs by a Portuguese singer, Amalia Rodriguez.

When he returned to France after the war, he frequented the Jewish youth club, and that was where he took notice of my mother. After my mother married Louis, Damien married a woman he had fallen for. They stayed together for a couple of years. No one ever knew what had happened between them, except that one day, he told her he was going to get a pack of cigarettes and never came back. He told me that story a few times, each time looking amused, vindictive, and proud.

After he heard that my parents had separated, he looked my mother up and began courting her. In my grandmother's eyes, Damien was the perfect suitor for her daughter; a Sephardic Jew from a good family, good-looking, well-educated, and responsible, with an air of authority about him. Damien was working at his brother's steel and iron business which was booming as post-war Europe was being rebuilt.

But Damien, unable to take orders from anyone and used to having things his way, quit the family business and decided to open his own iron and steel company. With funding from his mother and sisters, he opened "Les Aciéries de la Seine" in the late 1950s. In the following decades, he became a very successful businessman. He was hard-working and willing to do any task his business required. He would rise at four o'clock in the morning and come back, quite often, well past nine in the evening.

*

I had met Damien a few times while in foster homes; he would accompany my mother on critical occasions. He was quiet and did not interact with me much. But he was there when they came to my rescue a couple of times, so I liked him. When they brought me back home to live with them, I thought of him as my savior.

But within a year, his domineering personality and the tyrannical rules he enforced in our household became unbearable. The apartment had to always be spick-and-span. When he came home at night, he would take his coat off and hang it, then slide his index finger over the top of the armoire next to the coat hanger, studying it intently to try and detect the presence of dust. When he did, an offended look would appear, cleaning had been sub-standard that day.

*

Damien was also very particular about the food he ate and how it had to be cooked. If it didn't live up to his expectations, he would put down his knife and fork and push away his plate in disgust, looking as if he had just swallowed something rotten. He only wanted to be served dishes he himself enjoyed, and regardless of my likes or dislikes, he would always order me to finish what was on my plate. When I disliked a particular food, he often forced me to have a second serving.

Once, at Sunday lunch, Reine served one of Damien favored entrées; it was a Greek dish with meatballs, okra, and tomato sauce. I had tasted okra before and had to spit it all out. On the outside, okra was rough to the tongue, kind of prickly, and on the inside, it had a slimy consistency that made me gag. When Reine tried to serve me, I moved my plate away reflexively.

"Put your plate back on the table," my mother said, and she served me a good portion.

I put a tiny piece of the vegetable in my mouth and tried to swallow it as fast as possible without chewing on it, hoping I would not feel the slime, but it did not work.

"Yuck!" I blurted out in disgust.

Damien looked up. "If you are so disgusted, keep it to yourself!" he exclaimed angrily. "And you will eat what is on your plate, period!" I looked at my plate, felt a chill going down my spine, and said, "I can't."

Damien stopped eating, put his fork and knife down gently on the table, and still sitting, pushed his chair back a little, like someone planning to stand up. But he did not. Instead, his hypnotic gray eyes trapped mine, and I could not look away. He wanted me to watch. Extending his arms, not releasing his gaze from my frightened eyes, he unlocked his gold cufflinks, placed them on the table, and slowly rolled up his impeccable light blue shirt sleeve. He rolled up the fabric with care, one fold at a time, watching my eyes fill with terror.

I was hypnotized, immobile, barely breathing. By the time Damien began to work on his left sleeve, the terror was too much; suddenly, I broke the spell, disengaged my eyes, slipped down from my chair, ran full speed to the bathroom, and locked myself in. I wondered if he could find a way through the door. Maybe he had special powers like the ones I had heard about in scary ghost stories the foster kids had shared. Luckily, he didn't.

The family dynamics were difficult for me to handle. During the years we spent apart, the mother I knew early in my childhood had been erased, replaced by a woman I did not recognize and did not like. I felt I had nothing in common with her any longer. I would cringe with displeasure when someone talking about me would exclaim with a smile and good intentions, "Oh! She looks so much like her mom!"

Even though I felt distant from my mother, I was happy to be back home because it meant that I could finally go to school. School had started four months before, but I seemed to adjust very well; I already knew how to read and write. It allowed me to feel at ease with the other kids in my class; they were nice to me, and so was the teacher, who smiled a lot. No one seemed displeased with me. It was so unusual that it felt a bit strange at first.

But the whole atmosphere was welcoming and comforting. I loved the smell of the wooden desks and benches, the large window opening onto the small Parisian Street. I would sometimes rest my head, cheek against the desktop, close my eyes, and breathe deeply, my nostrils wide open like I had seen animals do. Then I would open my eyes and look out the window, watching the big clouds floating across the sky while listening and not missing even one of the teacher's words.

Soon school became my safe place, and unlike other children, I loved Mondays, as going back to school was the only way out of the apartment and the feeling of dread which was now constant at home. I feared Sundays the most because Damien was around the entire day.

One afternoon, I ran around the house, pretending to fly. I made humming and buzzing noises to imitate the sounds powerful engines made when a plane flew overhead. They looked so tiny up there, but they were mighty loud, nonetheless. I had been told to calm down and be quiet, but my enthusiasm prevailed. When Damien appeared in the doorway, I instantly stopped, frightened by the irritation I saw on his face.

He grabbed my arm so forcefully that it hurt. I screamed and kicked him, trying to free myself as he pulled me into the bathroom, sat on the toilet seat, and threw me face down across his lap. Then I felt my panties being pulled down, and the burning humiliation of my nakedness enraged me so much that, with all the strength I could muster, I yanked myself out of his grasp and got up while pulling my panties back up.

"You have no right to touch me! You're not my father!" I screamed.

I ran to my room and hid under the bed. I was seething from head to toe, wrapped in a blanket of unrestrainable rage. I could feel the humiliation underneath my skin, in every square millimeter of my body, but I could not let him see it. I stayed hidden, trying to catch the meaning of the muffled voices coming from the next room, but I could not make out the words. I could only hear tones: Damien's furious and accusatory, my mother's soothing and attempting to appease his bruised ego.

*

From that day on, things changed around the house.

As we sat down to eat, Damien would inspect the table I had been ordered to set with impeccable geometry. With a frown on his forehead, he looked suspicious as if he expected to find an ugly stain on the white tablecloth. He never looked pleased, and he never showed appreciation for a well-done job. On the other hand, he never failed to express his displeasure whenever he felt justified.

Each evening, after clearing the table, I stood alone in the kitchen, feeling overwhelmed by the amount of work I had to do. I had to clean the dishes first, being careful not to bang them against each other so as not to disturb my stepfather's sensitive ears. When I was done with the washing up, it was time for me to clean Damien's, Reine's, and my own shoes. I had become an expert at polishing and shining shoes in the precise way he had taught me.

Because Damien was handling metal covered in thick, dirty grease at work, the first step was to remove all oily matter from the leather with a turpentine-soaked cloth. Then it was time to take out the brown polish and spread it with another cloth on the leather, but not before removing the shoelaces that needed to be washed separately in soap and hot water. The clean laces were laid to dry on the floor while I continued my work.

I would wipe away the excess polish with a third cloth and begin to buff the shoe. A perfect sheen would appear as I brushed the shoe, first the sides and all around, working my way to the heel, the tip, and the top. Finally, I would weave the shoelaces back into their holes and put the shoes away for the night. It was only then, at around nine o'clock, that I was allowed to return to my room. After doing my schoolwork, I went to bed, often crying myself to sleep.

One night, I was awakened from a dream by a hand tightly gripping my shoulder and shaking me until I sat up. It was dark outside, but I could see Damien's silhouette against the faint light glowing from the next room.

"Follow me," he said; his unpleasant tone made me wish I was deaf. "I have something to show you."

I followed him to the shoe cabinet. He asked me to pull his shoes out, and I obeyed, frightened, then looked up at him, not understanding what had made him so mad.

"Look at them!" he ordered in his oh-so-quiet voice.

I looked but could not see anything. "Here, here, and here!" He pointed at the heels and the tip of the shoes. "Did you really think I was not going to notice?!"

I was quiet; I still could not see what had made him so upset. "This is the work of a lazy pig," he said, happy to demean me once again. He ordered me to go back to the kitchen, start over and do it right this time. I obliged, and when all done, I went back to bed but could not sleep, hating him with all my might.

*

Soon, my relationship with Damien became even more fraught with resentment.

Once a month on a Friday, I brought home my report book to be signed by my parents and returned to the teacher on Monday morning.

I had come to regard this book as a sacred object. It inspired fear and respect in me. I was afraid that it could be accidentally stained or, worse, lost. Returning to school without the book was unthinkable. Each weekend I spent with my book at home, I checked my school bag a hundred times to ensure it was still there. I only felt truly reassured when I handed it back, signed, to my teacher. To this date, it had happened without fail.

It was Sunday evening. So, I went to my room, knelt, opened my bag, feverishly searched, and found the brown cardboard book. I glanced at it, hoping that by some miracle, the zero I had received for misbehaving in class had disappeared. Unfortunately, it was still there, right in the middle of the page, impossible to miss.

I walked back to the corridor where my mother and my stepfather were standing; they were in the middle of an argument, both sounding very upset. At first, they did not notice me. I was afraid of interrupting them, but postponing was now out of the question. I gently pulled my mother's skirt to attract her attention. While continuing the conversation, Reine took the report book from me.

Silence fell as my mother went over the two pages where the notes and comments from teachers were recorded. I knew that these pages had the power to trigger unexpected reactions such as a smile, furrowed brows announcing an imminent storm, or scathing remarks. I feared that the wrath of hell would rain down on me if a perfectly round but utterly terrible zero sat there written in red ink. I felt that these zeros had a life of their own. They were so dominating, somehow erasing all the good grades that preceded and followed them.

My mother did not say a word and just brusquely handed the book to Damien. I scrutinized their faces trying to anticipate their upcoming reactions.

My stepfather took his time. He must have read the pages at least twenty times. The air thickened all around, the atmosphere became unbearable, and I felt it was hard to breathe. Finally, he raised his head and threw a stern look at me. I tried to escape his piercing stare, but I could not move. I was immobilized and yet fascinated by the look in those eyes; I knew that something terrible was about to happen.

My eyes widened with disbelief as I saw him slowly shake the book a little. Then there was an unreal tearing sound as he ripped it to pieces, his eyes riveted to mine.

Shreds of the sacred schoolbook floated in the air and fell softly to the ground one after another like feathers. Not for a moment did his eyes leave mine. The satisfaction that he felt watching my quiet fear was palpable. Did he hope to see me cry or run and try to stop him? I did not make a move. I did not say a word. Only my eyes were screaming.

I shut my eyes so that the monster would not win, so he would not see that he was hurting me so badly. I was overtaken by chaos, fear, dizziness. My heart was pounding loudly; my throat was dry. There was no way to run from the thoughts which raced through my mind like a series of lightning strikes: no more school, nowhere to go, no way out, no way to stay alive. I no longer felt my body. I disappeared into a black hole until finally, I showed no sign of life; I was a stone statue, white and icy.

My mother started to scream at her husband. My frozen expression must have frightened her. There was anguish on her face. She grabbed my shoulders; her lips were moving.

It was too late. I wanted to be dead. *Please let me die.*

"We'll tell the teacher it was an accident," my mom said. "We'll glue all the pieces together with tape, all the pieces to the last one. I'll explain everything. Are you listening to me?" By then, she was screaming. "Can you hear me? I promise you! Now go on, go and wash your hands; it's time for dinner."

Suddenly, her voice had stopped being an endless series of meaningless sounds.

That evening, after dinner, my mother stayed up late and glued back together all the pieces of the schoolbook. I wrapped myself in my blankets and kept my eyes open for a long, long time. I knew I would never forget Damien's look, his sadistic pleasure mixed with hate, his eyes coming alive with the desire to cause pain, to hurt beyond words, beyond screams, beyond tears.

~ REFLECTIONS & INSIGHTS ~

Damien's evil eyes had reminded me of Madame Valcourt's and the aversion I had read in them. And now, I lived trapped under the net of his despising blue-gray eyes on me. Drop by drop, his unrelenting expression of disgust instilled a poison into my bloodstream that distorted my perception of myself. It led me to believe that I was ugly; it made me feel dirty. For many years, the adult I became looked for ways to overcome the self-image that tortured her. But no matter what, I kept seeing myself through his eyes. This was insidious, inescapable. It distorted and overpowered the image reflected in the mirror.

The times Madame Valcourt lost her temper, adrenaline rushed and swirled mercilessly inside of me. Terror possessed me. Crouching behind my bed offered no protection, I was trapped with nowhere to flee, the only option left was to fight with all my might.

With my stepfather, I reacted differently. I had been around him for almost a year by now. I often feared and shrank away from his magnetic eyes that wouldn't let go of mine. Hiding was the only way I knew to break the spell until his attention was elsewhere.

The day he tore my schoolbook to pieces, there was no running away from the consequences of what he had done. It was the end of life as I knew it. I was spellbound, shell-shocked, immobilized, floating outside and away from my body. I was unreachable, untouchable, and the terror and the screams in my head finally stopped.

CHAPTER XI

Let Me Help You Breathe

IN THE SUMMER of 1959, Damien rented a house in the country, about sixty miles from Paris. His sisters, their husbands, nieces, nephews, and his father reunited under one roof. The family welcomed the opportunity to get away from the city's oppressive heat and pollution.

The picturesque two-story house was in the middle of nowhere. Ivy had climbed high, almost entirely covering one of the cream-colored stone walls. Outside the perimeter, wheat fields stretched far and wide around the property, flanked in the distance by lines of leafy trees. A few miles away, a small village boasted a bakery, a butcher shop, and a grocery store.

For Damien and his family, getting together held promises of peace, sunshine, long lunches in the garden, and good company. However, I was not part of that company. I was outside, looking in.

I watched my cousins have fun with their uncle, but I was never invited to join. His nieces and nephew saw Damien as the young, good-looking uncle they could always turn to, their role model; it flattered him; with them, he was relaxed; he smiled, played ping-pong, and went for bike rides. I had dreamed that Damien might like me as much someday, but it was hopeless. He hardly ever acknowledged my presence.

When he looked at me, I wished I could magically turn invisible. His blue eyes seemed to change color, turned gray, and became hard, his smile was gone, and aversion was written all over his face. There had to be an explanation for this; something had to be seriously wrong with me. I began to believe what I read in his eyes reflected the reality of who I was and how I appeared to the world, not just him.

I spent time in the garden, hiding behind tall bushes and trees. I would dig in the dirt, look for worms, then cut them into slices. I did not think of the worms as living beings then; they were just things that squirmed and looked disgusting. Freud, I am sure, would have seen that as an attempt to "castrate" Damien, but I think I was just identifying with them and attempting to destroy the repulsiveness I felt about myself.

I would torture a doll I had found in the dirt, grab her by the feet, and smash her head repeatedly onto the stone wall of the property. I would throw her in the air, tell her I would catch her but watch her fall to the ground, unaware that I was reenacting the betrayal inflicted upon me. I would pull her hair and talk to her in the same low-toned voice and barely contained rage Damien used when addressing me. I feared being discovered; but I could not help but hate that doll, just as much as I hated Damien.

The solace nature had offered me, the hope that my mother's love was not lost and that she would come to my rescue had carried me through some of the worst times of my short life, but not anymore. My senses were becoming blunted. The world was ignoring me, so I tuned it out. I floated away, almost lost for good, and no one noticed.

One evening, as I stood in the half-light at the back of the garden, Damien and his father stepped out of the kitchen through the back door, deep in animated conversation. I was too far from them to make out the words. Instinctively, I ducked behind a bush, knelt, and listened.

Grandpa spoke with authority. He sounded distraught. In contrast, Damien's voice was sheepish, a tone I had never heard from him before. As they came closer to my hideout, my ears perked up. I could hear the words spoken with acute clarity. "No one should treat a child the way you treat Taja! It's unacceptable! She is a little kid, and you're a grown man. I did not raise you to be a bully! What's wrong with you?" Grandpa exclaimed.

I could hardly believe what I had just heard. No one had ever spoken to Damien that way.

Damien remained quiet as they walked away, but I could still detect shock and disappointment in Grandpa's tone.

Something melted away inside me and I slid down to the ground. The earth was cool, tears began to roll down my cheeks, and I was back in the balm of the evening. *I am not alone! Grandpa! Grandpa!* Sitting in the twilight, I sobbed, cleansing tears. Then I heard a door open, and a voice called out my name. It was time for dinner.

As I entered the kitchen, Reine was sitting at the large table while a freshly made vegetable soup was being served. She had been feeling overwhelmed by the hormonal changes of pregnancy. She was now in her seventh month, and her belly was big. By mid-afternoon, the hottest part of the day, she endured severe panic attacks as she struggled to breathe, convinced that she was suffocating.

The aunts were fussing around her, which did not seem to help. I watched her from afar, laboring to get air in. After a while, the crisis would pass, and she would calm down. She would cry deeply, quietly, then be helped to a shaded chaise longue, lie down, sigh, and fall asleep for a while. I remember aching for her kind glance, feeling I was the cause of her distress, yet desperate for a comfort I felt I did not deserve.

Well into August, Damien had announced he would take a trip back to Paris for a few days; he needed to take care of something at work. He left on the weekend accompanied by Ino, who was his bookkeeper and brother-in-law. Ino and Lina, Damien's youngest sister, had a daughter, Jacqueline. She was the only "cousin" my age, but most of the time, she was glued to her mother, and we rarely spent time together.

On the night the two men left, we were eating cherry pie when Jacqueline turned to her mom and asked, "Maman, can I sleep with you tonight?"

Her mother nodded her approval with a smile and a caress on her daughter's cheek. This prompted me to ask my mom to stay with her that night. To my surprise, she agreed.

My mother's bed was exquisitely comfortable, covered with fresh-smelling, thick, white cotton sheets, and atop a soft and silky dark red bedcover, stuffed with down, light as a cloud, a perfect shield from the chill of the night. My head resting on a plump pillow, I looked at my mother, beautiful in her long-sleeved white gown, as she walked into the room, sat in front of the dressing table, and began to brush her long auburn hair, seemingly absorbed by her reflection in the mirror. After climbing in with difficulty, holding her round belly, she kissed me good night and switched off the light. I turned to my side and buried my nose into my mother's hair, breathing in that heavenly scent that, to this day, I can still feel tickling my nostrils. It had been a long time since I had been that close to her. With a smile on my face, I escaped to dreamland.

A terrible crash shook the house in the middle of the night, waking most of its occupants. The adults got up, sure that a drunk driver had run his car into the garage wall at the road's edge. What else could have made such an explosive bang?

They went out to check, but the garage wall was intact. They then checked the kitchen and other rooms but found nothing; baffled but unable to solve the mystery at this late hour, everyone went back to bed.

After breakfast, it was time to clean. Jacqueline and I were in charge of cleaning the room we shared, so, armed with a dustpan and broom, I walked to our room and opened the door. The door was so dark I could barely see the floor. I was barefoot and stepped on something gritty that should not have been there. I dropped the broom to the floor, gingerly walked to the window, and opened the tall shutters to let the sunshine in. I turned around and gasped at what I saw.

The cot with my blue sleeping bag on top was set against the back wall opposite the window. Hanging from the wall above my pillow, there had been an imposing old painting in a massive, gilded frame with intricate carvings. But now, my cot was littered with its broken pieces. The lower part of the frame was buried at an odd angle in my pillow, while the top had come to rest on my sleeping bag, now covered in white dust.

I walked out of the room on rubbery legs and bumped into Aunt Lina. I grabbed her hand and led her back to the room. She took one step inside, saw the damage, and called out for the others to come and see.

The mysterious incident involving the painting made me remember a similar instance when my aunt Rose gave Reine an unusually shaped, colorful ceramic vase that stood on three feet. When he saw the vase, Damien looked insulted - I could almost see his brain plotting revenge against it, looking for a way to make the hideous thing disappear. Before long, it came to him to place the vase with one of its three feet halfway off the shelf. When it fell and smashed according to plan, he said: "It was an accident!" giving me a side-long look and a wry smile, squinting to avoid the smoke of the cigarette in the corner of his mouth.

Later, I wondered if my fate was to end up like the vase. His smile was terrifying.

~ REFLECTIONS & INSIGHTS ~

I turned my attention inward as Jonty asked how I was feeling.

"The word 'lonely' comes to mind ... I wish someone would hold my hand ..." I thought about my mom that summer, I saw myself looking at her from afar, watching her midafternoon breathing episodes, "I wanted her to take my hand, like Madame Pomaré used to, my kind and smiling old friend. She was like a fairy godmother. I can see her so clearly. I crave her peaceful garden, her gentle touch."

I remembered the endless lunches outside, the warm weather, our friendship. There, I was not alone, I was a happy child, sad sometimes though.

"I need soothing so much ... I need her hand upon my shoulder ..."

Jonty said, "Feel her hand upon your shoulder."

I dived into the pain of impossible loss. Madame Pomaré at first, then my mother ... Now sobbing like an inconsolable child, so many tears stored inside flowing out like a river. I screamed, "I'm scared, I'm scared! I'm so scared!! Maman!! Don't leave me, help me, SAVE ME!"

The despair and the tears were so intense now that my chest was ready to burst. I struggled to breathe, just like my mom had during that summer. *I can't breathe!* The terrifying sensation brought me back to the present.

"Jonty, I'm going to die, it's too much ... please don't let me die!"

"I won't let you die!" I trusted his words, the kindness in his voice reassuring. I descended into the terror of loss and the sensation of falling endlessly. Then my mother's face reappeared.

"When my mom was struggling to breathe, she wouldn't look at me, she was always looking away..."

"Ask her to look at you," Jonty said softly.

"Maman, look at me, I'm here. I'm all alone, Maman, I'm scared ..." As the river of tears continued to run down my cheeks, I pictured her face, her eyes, her hair - how she couldn't breathe ...

I imagined my eight-year-old self, coming out from behind the bushes, crossing over and kneeling in front of her, placing my hands on both her cheeks, making her look at me. My eyes plunged into hers; her beautiful but frightened light brown eyes are slowly focusing on me now. I see her, and she sees me. This intense belief comes over me that I have the power to soothe, to heal as I wrap her into my comforting voice: *"Breathe with me, Mamma, be with me, you and me together."* I am giving her all I needed from her, all of it. *"Look at me, I'll help you, I'm going to hold your belly. You can breathe now, see, I'm breathing with you, you'll be all right, we're all right, Mamma!"*

As I cried the deepest tears ever, I had this strange feeling of being so young and yet so strong for her. And then I pictured her holding me, my fear gone, and the sadness, deep, strong intense when I imagined helping her breathe better. "I wanted to take care of my Mamma ..."

It would have been us against the world. Just the two of us. Together.

~ INSIGHTS ~

This "Please look at me" feeling has run through my relationships. At that moment in the session when I begged my mom to look at me as I held her face in my hands, looked deep into her brown eyes, and helped her breathe, the shame was gone. When she saw me, it was like I was given the right to live, to exist despite my little brother coming.

I realized there were other times when the shame was gone, they all had to do with warmth and acceptance. Like when I left France, exhilarated by the crossing of the Atlantic Ocean, by California, its warm climate, easy lifestyle, and by new friendships and Primal Therapy, the pleasure of anticipated cleansing of body and soul. It was an adventure, an escape. Shame melted away, I began to feel beautiful and desirable then … maybe for the first time.

The days at the beach, the parties, the music, and dancing the warm nights away, all of it was intoxicating. I craved touch, I craved warm eyes on me. The delightful intimacy made me feel elated.

I've always loved looking into warm eyes. They were the antidote to the poison of my stepfather's gaze. I've also always loved holding hands; I can feel warmth emanating and penetrating mine.

Tears welled up from the depth of my heart, leading me back to an earlier summer when my family went camping. We never stayed anywhere for long. Again and again, I fell in love from afar with an older boy or a young man who never knew I even existed. A few days later, my parents would pack and leave, and each time we left I was heartbroken, sobbing in the back seat of the car, alone, while Reine and Damien ignored the sound of my despair, pretending I was not even there. They did not want me; they would not look at me, I was locked away behind an invisible wall, but *I* could see them and feel the cold stab of their intentional indifference.

It's no wonder I have zero tolerance for people lacking empathy, oblivious of other people's pain. How I despise people who hurt animals! They have no voice; they're vulnerable and easy to ignore, as I was then. I believe that's why our world is so damaged, broken, because of people who have lost the ability to take responsibility for the pain they inflict upon children, nature, and humanity.

The warmth of my father and Madame Pomaré feels like the warmth of the sun, and the agony caused by my foster mothers' and Damien's malice feel like the coldness of impending death. These two themes, as intertwined as the Gordian knot, drove my body, my perceptions, my mind, and my life. Without tenderness in my early life, I wouldn't have survived the later hatred. Without that experience of warmth, how could I even have known what I so desperately needed?

CHAPTER XII

That Old Yearning

~ REFLECTIONS & INSIGHTS ~

IN 1978, a new behavior emerged, it was a yearning so strong it turned into an addiction that drove me to be involved with several boyfriends simultaneously. At the time, I did not recognize it for what it was. It felt so comfortable to fall back into the familiar dating behaviors of the late 60s'.

In my sessions, as I dived back into the devastating immensity of abandonment and loss, I became overwhelmed by the feeling that this was a bottomless pit of pain that would never end.

Then one day, I was caught off guard by a remark a close friend made about my dating "style". I felt a tinge of embarrassment and in that moment, what had so far seemed to be natural began to feel not so normal after all. I knew then that it was time to explore the underlying motivation in my therapy sessions.

Then something unforeseen happened.

Occasionally, I had been taking Valium. But for a while, painful memories had been coming up, interfering with my ability to function well, so I took more. After a couple of months, I ran out and stopped. The withdrawal was so brutal that it caused me to have a series of grand mal seizures over an endless weekend. At some point my body continued to go into convulsions that were no longer seizures.

Fully conscious, I relived sequences of my struggle in the birth canal, after my mother's fall, pushing against the walls, kicking, hyperventilating for long minutes, then stopping, resting, and starting all over again.

I remember how incredibly right it felt, how every movement, every twist and turn, the rhythm, the intensity felt like it was me, the complete, untouched, undamaged, instinctual me. I felt I was following the exact path I needed to follow, moving as I needed, drawing unbelievable power and energy from the intensity of the breath, my body feeding on it, energized by it, stronger because of it. Remarkably, re-experiencing these birth sequences freed me from much of my emotional vulnerability.

When I recovered and I went back to work, I felt a noticeable change in me. I felt good in my skin, healthy, but more importantly, I felt strong. My new behavior seemed to match that early experience in the birth canal of being whole, undamaged, with a new sense of myself that made me feel anchored in the present reality, solid, finely tuned into it. The way I related to those around me felt different too. I was comfortable, happy to be in agreement when I was, and unapologetic when I was not. I would not recommend a Valium rebound to anyone, but it certainly pushed me beyond the limits of what I thought I could feel and gave me full access to the recorded memory of my birth. I truly re-connected to a part of my *self* I had lost after birth.

Although this series of primals had been the most healing experience ever, my instinct told me that there was more to uncover. Something big, still inaccessible, like an "invisible elephant in the room."

The immensity of the sadness and the terror I felt when life separated me from someone I loved was still there.

And finally, one day, as I once more re-visited the experience of my birth, the most violent, agonizing sensations came over me, a vertigo so unbearable I wished I could die right there and then. I was falling, falling. It felt like eternity. The terror shook me beyond any measurement on the Richter scale the moment I was grabbed by my feet and held upside down.

The elephant in the room was now in plain sight.

And I knew right then that Hell was Separation. Physiological, physical, and emotional.

That is when I fully grasped how the intensity of the despair and terror I felt when I was abandoned had been layered upon that original imprint of the brutal physiological and physical separation from my mother's body. *And that was why*, with the depth of the unbearable sadness of loss came the sensation of a fall with no end, and with it, a sense of immeasurable horror and terror. Wordless, because the newborn has no words.

In a flash, I understood the reason for multiple boyfriends, why I had had no choice but to safeguard and protect myself from the deep despair that never failed to come up when I feared being abandoned. What I was really protecting myself from was the memory of that fall, the separation and sense of disintegration when I was held upside down. In that moment, I sensed I was dissolving, without the anchors that would have kept me safely grounded and prevented me from falling, from getting lost in space... I separated from my *self*, forever.

Just a few moments of such agony for a newborn create an imprint deeply buried yet all-powerful, more so than any of the hellish experiences that would come later.

It all comes together on so many levels. I was separated from my mother's womb; separated from my home, father, Madame Pomaré; separated by my stepfather with my mother's complicity from all the people I loved as a child, my real family; separated from my music, my guitar, and my beloved teacher.

From that day on I never felt the need for multiple partners.

CHAPTER XIII

Confusion & Misery

IT WAS IN NOVEMBER of 1959 that my brother, Adam, was born. By mid-November, the weather had turned cold and windy, the sky was low and dark, but I did not mind. I walked home from school rushing in joyful anticipation. My mother was about to come back home from the maternity clinic where she had stayed for a couple of weeks. I was going to meet my baby brother!

As I entered our building, I heard loud voices and laughter coming from the upper floor. I knew it had to be all the uncles, aunts, and cousins who had come to meet Damien's first son. The old elevator dragged itself up at a snail's pace to the 5th floor. I could have jumped up and down with impatience. When it stopped with a final hiccup, I opened the door, got out, and ran toward the apartment.

The door was wide open, as the small apartment could not accommodate the crowd of visitors; a small group of guests had gathered past the threshold and into the hallway, talking animatedly while clinking their champagne flutes.

I fought my way to clear a path through the crowd, stopped here and there by an affectionate tap on my tousled hair. I was surrounded by a forest of well-dressed legs, pants and stockings, shiny shoes, and high heels. At the end of the long corridor, I entered the big living room.

The room was packed with people and flooded with lights. The familiar faces and the warmth in the air made this vast room feel like a safe place, a castle hidden and protected, as if beyond these walls, the world did not exist.

I felt dizzy for an instant and had a hard time spotting my mom.

When I finally saw her, I ran to her and threw myself into her arms. Reine seemed overwhelmed and a bit tense, but she was smiling. She grabbed my hand and pulled me toward a small crib where a minuscule being was resting, so ugly and blue it gave me a shock. I had never seen a tiny baby before, and I did not expect his little face to be all wrinkled. I had imagined my baby brother would look like a baby doll, round and pink, smiling with brown or blue eyes wide open.

My mom proudly introduced me:

"This is Adam!"

"But he is so ugly!" I uttered. The newborn looked like it had fought terrible battles and was now a very, very old person in pain, his fists and eyelids shut tight. My heart went out to him. I wished I could protect him from the invasive, loud chatter, and from the lights pouring down on him.

I do not remember what happened next, because soon after, I began to have a recurring nightmare that overpowered what had happened that day; in it, the story metamorphosed into a different one. That new story imposed a new ending that I could never erase.

As the dream begins, it is an exact replay of the actual day described above until the moment I looked at my baby brother and wished I could protect him.

The doorbell rings a few times.

"Darling, please go and open the door for me, will you?" Reine asks.

I do not want to leave the room but obediently walk away from the lights. In just a heartbeat, the atmosphere of this happy get-together changes. The corridor is now empty and turns very dark; the loud voices coming from the living room are barely audible now although I know the room is still packed with people.

As I follow the long corridor toward the entrance, I am overwhelmed by a sense of dread. When I reach the door, the bell rings again impatiently, almost angrily. I stand there, my heart beating fast, making too much noise. I do not want it to be heard. I do not want to open the door, but an irresistible force is pushing me. Chills run down my spine.

Very slowly, I open it inch by inch, just enough to peek outside. At first, I see nothing. As my eyes get used to the night, I see a hideous old witch facing me. She is all dressed in black. Her nose is hooked and covered with warts, and her back is hunched. She has a toothless smile and shiny, button-like black eyes. It is death standing on the landing.

I try to cry out in distress, to run, run away from the frightful creature. With all the strength I can muster, I attempt to withdraw from the power and influence this old woman has on me. She has come to take me away, far from here, far from my home, from my mamma forever, and no one is coming to my rescue. No one knows what was happening just a few feet away.

With all my might, I try to slam the door, but the more I try, the more I feel a pervasive weakness possess my entire body. The feeling of horror is intolerable. Suddenly, the ground under my shoes begins to move inexorably, expelling me from my home until I am almost outside the apartment, unable to scream, powerless to flee. As if it has a will of its own, the door suddenly pushes me out, slams itself shut and I hear the clicking sound of a key turning in the lock behind me. I am all alone now, kidnapped without a sound, without a word, without a sign left behind.

Each time, I would wake up shaken to the core. Death was coming so close, so fast, but I could not make a sign or say a word. I attempted to raise my arm but could not move a muscle. I would just lay there, paralyzed, unable to even open my eyelids. I would feel my breathing slow down, my chest almost motionless.

Each time it happened, I thought it was the end: first, the nightmare leaping out of the past, and then, the paralysis, the inability to act even in the face of mortal danger.

CHAPTER XIV

The Jerrican

IT WAS THE SUMMER of 1960. Damien was driving, and Reine sat next to him in the passenger seat. They seemed unusually relaxed, even happy. My baby brother, Adam, now nine months old, was sleeping nestled in a small basket next to me on the backseat. We were on our way to a campsite for the summer holiday near Le Lavandou, a town on the Mediterranean Sea. I enjoyed these long rides: nothing to do, free to escape, imagine new beginnings, planning, and re-inventing my life. I loved the feeling of floating away, my eyes half-closed, daydreaming about wild, faraway places.

It was sunny outside, and every once in a while, I would look out the window and take in the ever-changing scenery unfolding left and right of the road. In my mind's eye, I would photograph the flatlands, divided into deep green fields separated by tree-lined roads, some leading to small groups of old stone houses huddled together. Sometimes the flatlands turned into rolling hills. I imagined mystery and hidden places where one could walk and then lie down and rest, listen to nature's melodies, and let the wind be the guide to another safe hideaway.

Damien drove with confidence; I enjoyed his style; fast, resolute, daring, but in control. The engine purred, appreciative of the way it was handled. There was a rhythm, and sometimes when I paid attention, I heard music that I had never heard before. It seemed to come from another place, unknown to me; the melodic lines from each instrument interwove, soft and quiet in places, dramatic in others, and I felt uplifted, euphoric.

We drove until late in the afternoon and stopped at a hotel for the night. We ate fresh local fare at a restaurant for dinner, so there were no dishes to wash. But I felt like I needed to do something, so when we were done eating, I emptied all the plates into one, made a pile, and put all the knives and forks on top, ready for the waiter to pick up. When he arrived at the table, he smiled with surprise and appreciation. Damien clearly enjoyed my initiative. Was this a whisper of hope?

After a restful night, coffee, and fresh croissants in the hotel dining room, we climbed back into the car and rejoined the highway, hoping to make it down south by nightfall.

The campsite was a few miles inland, set in a forest of maritime pine trees. Their exquisite fragrance once again gave rise to a sense of home, hope, and belonging, magically erasing all traces of pain. It belonged within the world of my dreams. There, I was loveable; Damien and Reine cared about me. I felt elated as if this dream world was now my new reality. In it, I would change, I would do all I could, I would try passionately to become a daughter they could love.

The sun was low in the sky; the golden hour grew more vivid. It was that time of day when shadow and light seemed to reach an understanding and work together to offer the spectator a vision of intricate and meaningful beauty.

We drove up half a mile and reached the small piece of land that would be home for the month. Trees and wooden fences surrounded the parcel. It was flat in the middle with just enough room to tow and position the trailer. Damien maneuvered the car with difficulty, backing up, then moving forward again until he managed to place the trailer in the right spot.

The following day, Damien and Reine installed the awning, unfolded the table and chairs, and set up a makeshift outdoor dining room. Once our new living space was set up to Damien's satisfaction, he and I went to fetch water. We carried tall, square jerricans, which, when full, would hold about five gallons of water. Once a can was connected to a pipe inside the trailer, the toilet, the sink, and the mini shower would be operational.

The water station was a long way away, and as we walked across the campsite, we came into view of a spectacular swimming pool, its crystal clear blue-green water shimmering in the sunlight. People were lying around in brightly colored swimsuits, soaking up the sun with an expression of blissful delight on their red and tanned faces. Others were diving from a springboard, and kids were running around, jumping in, disappearing only to pop back up seconds later, soaked, energized, exhilarated.

It was a scorching day, and I could hardly wait until Damien gave me permission to join the fun. I felt intimidated a little, but the crystalline water was enticing, calling me; I would have been so happy to jump into it right then.

But we kept on walking to the water station. Damien filled the two water cans and carrying them like featherweights, retraced his steps. I walked alongside him, picking up my pace to catch up with his determined strides.

A few days went by. My chores were to sweep, dust the small trailer, and set the table for dinner. There was not much to do, but days passed, and we had not gone to the pool yet. Instead, we drove to the sea several times and settled on the sandy beach. I could hear distant laughter. Kids and teens ran along the shallow water, or further out until it got too deep to run; then, they would dive and swim away from the shore. The gentle ebb and flow of the Mediterranean rocked me into a dreamlike state.

I felt embarrassed to be seen walking all alone, friendless, so I hesitated but the appeal of the sea was irresistible. When I asked Reine if I could go swim, she nodded her consent halfheartedly.

"Don't go too far. I want to be able to see you at all times," she said.

I walked to the water's edge and stood there, savoring the warmth of the fine sand under my feet and the sun on my skin, oblivious of the noisy activity all around. I took one step forward, just enough for my toes to feel the water's caress. Then I walked straight into the sea, stopped when it reached my waist, waited for a minute, then jumped in. Buoyed up by the salty water, my body felt weightless. It made me feel clean; it washed away the pain and the shame.

I drifted away in the exquisite coolness of the sea, diving deep down, soothed, and awed by the magic of the world underwater. I could have stayed there forever but looking up toward the shore, I saw my mother waving for me to return. I headed back in slow strokes, my body one with the translucent water. As I reached the shore and walked onto the sand, my curls dripping, skin shimmering, I felt like a new, cleansed version of myself.

My baby brother was asleep in the shade of the navy-blue umbrella. I sat down, looked at him, took his tiny hand in mine and kissed it lightly. I would have loved to hold him, but I was not allowed. So, I sat there, next to him, legs folded up, my arms encircling them, listening to the buzzing sounds all around; then I lay down and curled up, slowly disconnecting myself from the noise until it faded away.

A couple more days passed, and we still had not gone to the swimming pool. I kept asking, but Damien kept refusing. Something I did or forgot to do must have displeased him. He had reverted to his old self, like when we were at home behind closed doors.

One day he ordered me to take an empty jerrican and refill it alone. I looked at him in disbelief, but he stood tall in front of me, resolute. I was afraid I could not do this alone, but there was no other option. I grabbed the big can half my size and started walking toward the water station.

I passed the swimming pool, longing for friends, wishing I could drop the jerrican by the side of the road and join in, carefree. But it was impossible, so I looked away and moved along. I finally arrived at my destination, placed the can under the faucet, and let the water run until it was full. I grabbed the handle with apprehension, but the can would not move. I tried again, and this time I managed to lift it off the ground for a second but had to let it go; it landed on the earth with a thud. It was too heavy.

I looked around, searching for a tool, something, anything that would help me prevail. Nothing. There was absolutely nothing.

I stood there, staring at the jerrican, wondering why Damien had sent me here alone. A thought suddenly struck me: it was so easy for Damien to lift the can, two of them even, that maybe he had not realized how heavy it would be for me. Happy with my discovery, I emptied the bottle halfway and lifted it. I began to walk back to the trailer, stopping here and there to enjoy the scent of the pine and sit on the carpet of needles. When I reached the spot where the path paralleled the swimming pool, I looked the other way, continued walking, and finally made it back.

Damien was sitting in an armchair, reading the newspaper. Without looking at me, he told me to deposit the can next to the others, but as I walked past him, he noticed that the jerrican was only half full.

"What is this?" he asked, his voice low and calm, a tone I feared and hated. He pointed his index finger at the can. "You could not be bothered to bring a full can back, could you?"

He stared at me with that look that made me feel dirty and ashamed.

"It was too heavy," I said in a small voice. "I couldn't carry it."

"You are going back right now!" he exclaimed. "And do not bother to come back unless it is full," he said, sending me on my way with an empty can.

I turned away and began to walk slowly toward the water station. Something was happening inside, and it was frightening. I was cold, seized by an almost irresistible impulse to escape, to run so far away that he could never find me, talk to me, look at me again. But I did not know where to run.

I focused all my attention on the sun's warmth on my back and the scenery, taking in shapes, colors, and scents. The sky was so blue it made me want to cry. I walked on with a lump in my throat, and my head started to hurt a little, but I finally made it to my destination, filled the water can until it overflowed, twisted the cap back on, and tried to lift it. I couldn't.

I stared at it, walked around it, and tried to pick it up a few times. Maybe if I held the handle with my right hand and leaned to my left, I could manage a few steps, then let the bottle down, pick it up again and move a few more steps. I practiced it for a while, and when my hand hurt too much, I switched sides, used my left hand, and leaned my body to the right, looking like a broken doll.

Soon, I had to stop because I felt dizzy. The tears I could not shed were suffocating me; the weight of the can was like a punishment. I glanced at the thick carpet of pine needles on the ground further up on the side of the road, and an idea emerged. The needles and the leaves came to my rescue, offering a sliding floor for the can that made the task manageable. I barely needed to lift, just pull and slide the jerrican. The thick carpet of needles cooperated. I had to look back every so often, so I would not trip, but my system worked. When I encountered an obstacle, I would drag the dead weight back to the sandy road, gather my strength and move along to the next stretch of pine needles.

From that day on, every so often, Damien sent me to get water. The shame burned me from inside, especially when passing the swimming pool. It felt like everyone was looking at me like an outcast;

everyone knew something was wrong with me. That must have been the reason why no one ever came to help.

~ REFLECTIONS & INSIGHTS ~

That morning, I felt uncomfortable at the hotel pool, disapproved of, as though I was an interloper, unwelcome. I tried to shrug it off and went swimming anyway, but I couldn't shake the feeling.

In my session, I told Jonty about it. "I felt they ignored me, that they didn't like me." He encouraged me to say more, so I described the scene, eliciting details my mind had recorded without even realizing it. The family playing together and splashing in the pool didn't look at me. The older man in a recliner never looked up from his newspaper. The woman reading a book glanced at me, and I thought I saw her roll her eyes. And the kids who ran past me screaming seemed to resent my presence.

"How did that make you feel?"

"I felt forlorn. I wanted them to smile and welcome me, but there were no smiles. It brought a lump to my throat. "

Jonty said, "Feel their gaze upon you!"

As I did so, I began to cry. *Why don't you like me? What's wrong with me?* The palm of my hands felt tender and hot. I watched my fingers curl around an imaginary handle and felt burning. My hands looked smaller, younger as if they had traveled back in time. The sensations unlocked a memory from long ago when we were camping in the Côte d'Azur. Another pool, filled with joyful holidaymakers. I saw them through my tears, all preoccupied with each other. My back began to ache a little at first and then much more. The physical pain reinforced the emotional; the feeling that something was wrong with me made me cry deeper.

My stepfather's tanned face, his eyes a striking deep blue gray, flashed in my mind's eye. I was walking alongside him when we went to the water station and returned. Then I stood before him, looking down as he commanded me to fetch the water.

At that moment in the session, I looked up at him with a sliver of hope, gone in a nanosecond.

I sobbed as I dragged the jerrican over the pine needles while begging Damien not to hate me *so much* ... I reached the pool. I did not want to look; stabbing pain was climbing along my spine, my legs too weak to walk, engulfed by shame.

I did not want to remember. I thought of dying right there and then. But I knew what I had to do this time, so I turned toward the happy people by the pool and called out, *"Please, it's too heavy! It hurts; please help me carry it!"* The crying was now convulsive, and the deeper it went, the easier it became to beg them from the bottom of my eight-year-old heart.

I was rewriting the story, watching a kind man and his two girls walking toward me. He smiled at me and picked up the jerrican. I cried out my despair, and when the feeling ended, the shame had melted away.

The redrafted story brought solace and dialectic where there was none.

SUMMER OF PEACE

Five years later, I got a taste of what life could be like away from my tormentor, Damien. A glimpse at the possibility of freedom. We were on another summer holiday with my family in the country, but this time accompanied by my stepcousin Jacqueline and her mother.

Jacqueline's big brown eyes, and her perfectly shaped nose were spoiled by the jealous expression she often had that emphasized her thin lips and revealed a darker side - something difficult to describe but very disquieting that I was wary of. This expression never surfaced that summer, and I knew that for the time being she was harmless.

We were both fifteen. For two months, we spent every minute of every day together, we ate together, we slept in the same room. Our days were occupied by long bike rides on winding country roads, flanked on either side by fields of wheat that spread as far as the eye could see. I remember waking up when a ray of sun reached my pillow and getting up to look out the window, my eyes immersed in the deep blue of the sky, watching the wispy clouds as they drifted across it. I remember the lazy afternoons spent in the sun, eating salads and fresh fruits, savoring every bite. Jacqueline's mom, Lina, and Reine did the cooking and the washing up, so my schedule that summer was chore free. I hardly ever saw Damien who was away working in Paris for long periods of time, sometimes accompanied by Jacqueline's dad, Ino.

Jacqueline and I had made a pact to lose weight and look our best by the end of the summer. So, diet, exercise and getting a tan were on top of our list. We both became borderline anorexic, but we loved our rejuvenated bodies. These were the days when being skinny was the fashion ideal, something to be worn with pride and delight.

I enjoyed her company, and little by little, my feelings for her began to change from initial distrust and unease to acceptance, closeness, and an intimate friendship that grew and strengthened over the long summer weeks.

Jacqueline's skin was turning a uniform deep dark brown. I was eating raw carrots in the hope of matching the color of her skin, but never did, no matter how much beta carotene I ingested. I turned golden, with a sprinkle of freckles on my nose, with long curly blond hair bleached by the sun.

Once, during a long bike ride, Jacqueline exclaimed, "Taja, you must enter the MAT competition. You could really win, you know."

MAT was short for "Mademoiselle Âge Tendre", a magazine for teenage girls. Each year, a 16-year-old was elected Miss MAT. The winner would be featured in the magazine, win a trip to New York, and an impressive number of other exciting gifts: a car, a television set, a refrigerator, a record player, a radio, a camera, books and records, a bicycle, a scooter, complete camping gear, a full summer and winter wardrobe, along with jewelry, watches, and beauty products.

I thought about what she had said. For a moment, my stepfather's frown flashed through my mind. It disrupted my peaceful, tranquil mood induced by the summer heat, Jacqueline's companionship, and the scents and sounds of the countryside all around us. But then my hand let go of the bicycle handle and waved away the troubling image so that I could focus on her idea.

It was not the attention that was tempting. It was the gifts and what they would make possible: I could break away from Damien, and I would have the freedom to control my own world, to feel as I did in that very moment. I could almost touch the dream, the never-ending adventure that was already forming in my mind, projected to a time so distant it looked just like the edge of the horizon I was taking in, a blur of blonds, blues and greens faded by the rising haze of heat.

We kept on riding until we reached a grove of trees. There, we parked our bikes under branches heavy with leaves of assorted shapes and greens. Our backs leaning against a big tree trunk, we rested, and drank fresh water that had become lukewarm in the sun, and just listened to the ceaseless buzzing of insects busy sustaining life in the nearby fields.

After some minutes, I interrupted our silence.

"Do you really think I could win?" I asked.

Jacqueline nodded, looking down at a small juicy apricot she was about to bite into. It was brightly colored against her dark skin. She broke it in half and handed me a piece.

"You can definitely win," she said while munching the fruit's sweet flesh.

"And what would we do with all that stuff?" I wondered out loud.

"Maybe we could sell what we don't need," she replied.

Although our teenage dreams never saw the light of day, that summer of joy and wellbeing stays with me to this day.

CHAPTER XV

Music, A New Lifeline

SINCE THE AGE of seven, I had been begging my mother to enroll me in music school; I wanted to learn to play the guitar. I felt a kind of romantic attraction, a fondness, and an affinity for the instrument. Unlike other kids my age who fantasized about becoming rock stars, classical guitar had a pervasive, almost magnetic appeal to me. I would not give up asking, but Reine kept refusing.

However, when I was eight, she enrolled me in music school to learn to play the violin. In her early years with Damien, Reine listened to classical music and loved the awe-inspiring sounds of Yehudi Menuhin's violin. I grew up listening to music she often played on the old record player, symphonies, and concertos, particularly Mendelssohn's Violin *Concerto in E minor*, which I could almost sing by heart in its entirety, Tchaikovsky's *Concerto in D major* for violin and orchestra, Brahms, Albinoni's *Adagio*, Bach ...

Music filled our apartment with joy, drama, beauty, and peace. It was all so real. Music could be gentle, almost quiet, cry softly or sob deeply, and then explode with such power that would connect me to my own strength, even when I felt small and powerless. I was moved to tears and uplifted by the rainbow of emotions it expressed.

I still longed to learn classical guitar, but it did not look like I had much choice. It was the violin or nothing. So, I attended violin classes, practiced at home, and did well. The teacher thought I had potential. Early on, Reine was invested in my training and performance. But after a while, she became moody; she spent days in bed, in the dark, flying from anger to tears to exaltation in no time. I wondered, *had my love of music become a threat to her?* At the end of the year, Reine simply stopped taking me to violin classes, and it was never spoken of again.

Learning to play the guitar now seemed like a distant fantasy. As my dream vanished into thin air, I became frustrated and even more resentful of my mother.

*

When I turned 16, we moved from Paris to a suburban town on the west side and I was enrolled in a new school, the Lycée du Raincy.

On the first day, Damien drove me to the entrance to drop me off. As he parked the car, I saw the crowd of girls and boys, and I was stupefied. I had not realized that my new school was co-ed. As my previous school was a girls-only institution, I had had little contact with boys my own age. For an instant, the urge to fling the car door open and run like the wind flooded every cell in my body.

"I don't know anyone!" I told Damien in a whisper to contain the turmoil inside.

"You'll make friends in no time," he replied with confidence and a genuine half-smile.

"I can't go in there!" I continued, hoping we would drive away.

"You must go in!" he replied, firm but unusually sympathetic.

Strangely, at that moment, the boys across the street terrified me. In contradiction, the presence of my stepfather in the car with me felt like I was home safe. For a moment, I focused on the delicate scent of his perfume that I had always loved.

I gave him a sheepish look, a kiss on the cheek, got out of the car, and from the corner of my eye, I watched him speed away. On the other side of the street, clusters of students were waiting for the gates to open. Many seemed to know each other well, reuniting after the long summer holiday, happy to catch up on the latest news and adventures. I stood there, embarrassed, unsure what to do with myself, and too frightened to speak to anyone.

As time went by, the unease faded away. I began to relax in this new environment. I became friends with George, a boy in my class who also lived in Noisy and traveled on the same train to and from school. We were happy to share the 20-minute ride from one destination to the other. I found out that he was attending music classes in Noisy, which boasted a small *conservatoire*. He aspired to become a famous conductor, which was all that mattered to him.

On a sunny, cold winter afternoon, we returned to Noisy earlier than our scheduled time. George offered to take me for a tour of the *conservatoire* and introduce me to the teachers there. I was not due home for another couple of hours, so without hesitation, I followed him.

He stopped in front of a small stone building on the left of the avenue, at the end of a long upward slope. There was a rusty metal gate that opened onto a small garden. I heard muffled music, the thunder of the drums, the discordant screeching of a bow on a violin's strings, the deep melodic voice of a cello coming from the upper floors.

George took me upstairs to one of the classrooms. The door was open, and a guitar player was practicing. I stood in the doorway, mesmerized by how he made the guitar weep. He sounded and looked like a being from a lost time, an otherworldly place. Indeed, he must have been to play like that.

Before long, he noticed us standing there in the doorway and stopped playing. The beautiful man asked me a question, but as I tried to answer, no words came out. I was so embarrassed I wished I could evaporate like a genie. But he just laughed kindly; he was not mocking me at all. Eventually, the three of us sat down, and I expressed my desire to be able to play "like that." He told me I could attend a class the next day. Several students in his two-hour class kept the cost so low that I could use my pocket money to cover it myself. I signed up at once, and he said goodbye and resumed his playing. As George and I walked home, I could still hear his guitar's otherworldly sounds ringing in my ears.

Back home, I told Damien and Reine about the music school. They did not object as long as I did not let my lessons and practice interfere with my academic performance. It was a reasonable request that I was happy to comply with. From then on, once – and sometimes twice – a week, I would attend my guitar class.

In the past, I had discarded my hope to play the guitar as an unrealistic fantasy but now, I fell in love desperately, and there was no stopping me. While my school friends were listening to the Beatles, I was listening to my hero, Andrés Segovia. I would practice every chance I had, knowing I was at risk of losing everything if Damien suddenly felt like reasserting his power over my life. I was careful not to show my enthusiasm and often waited until Reine and Damien left for the evening to see a movie or a play or eat out at a restaurant, which happened quite frequently. As soon as the front door closed behind them, I would jump out of bed, grab my guitar, and practice for hours until I heard the elevator. Only then would I hide the guitar under my bed, turn off the lights, and pretend to be asleep, in case they came in to check on me. They never did.

Life went on; I enjoyed going to school and the company of my new friends, but I began looking forward to going back home to play. Surprisingly, my mother let me be. Her hostility towards me seemed to subside, maybe because she enjoyed it when I played the chords and sang the lyrics of songs by her favorite artists. At dinner parties I would even be called upon to perform a couple of classical pieces for our guests who listened attentively while sipping cognac or other digestifs. Damien and Reine perfectly impersonated the proud and supportive parents they were not.

A TURBULENT YEAR

While I was happily lost in the world of music, I had no clue that the world out there was on the brink of a revolution. Damien and Reine seemed uncharacteristically content. I had passed my academic exam brilliantly and I believe they felt it reflected well on them in the eyes of the world. The atmosphere at home seemed to change for the better.

It was in the first days of May that Damien told us to pack our bags; we were leaving Noisy to go to his sister Lili's country home in Fontainebleau, isolated from the rest of the world, furnished just enough to accommodate the family's get-togethers on weekends. There was no radio or television.

Over the years, we had spent many weekends in Fontainebleau with Damien's family, and I had always been reluctant to go. However, this time was different. I was allowed to bring my guitar and practice to my heart's content. I wondered what had prompted my stepfather to be so tolerant of my playing.

It is almost impossible to imagine that as the student riots of *May 68* were unfolding, I was just miles away in complete ignorance.

The use of force against students only inflamed the political tension. Before long, high school students and an increasing number of young workers joined in. More and more people were hurt in the battles between police and students in the Latin Quarter. Eventually, the student unrest and the workers' strikes rolled across the country. The millions of workers on strike brought France to its knees, paralyzing its economy. But May 1968 came and went. By the end of June, a referendum reasserted De Gaulle's power. Apparently, the world had gone back to normal.

The impact of the student protests in 1968 would be felt for decades. Although the rebellion did not manage to end the current political era and Gaullism prevailed, it did change the way young people perceived the world, and it heightened their social awareness. I witnessed it the following year when I became part of the change. For me, fighting the establishment was closely related to fighting my repressive family, and this time I had allies all around me.

*

My wish to become a guitar player grew into a conviction in a few short months. I was sure that music would be my life, that I would become a professional player and travel the world to give concerts, just like Andrés Segovia did. I made a life-changing decision, and I needed to share it with someone, or I would burst.

Whenever he was free after class, my teacher would give extra time, one on one. We would sit opposite each other, and he would play. Hypnotized, I watched his fingers dance along the fretboard, listening to the beautiful sounds coming from his instrument, lost in unfamiliar nuances.

Sometimes he showed me how to play a melody, and we would play together; the marriage of the two guitars was always a highlight and an inspiration. From time to time, he would hand me his guitar so I would experience what it was like to play a professional instrument. Playing then felt almost effortless, my fingers barely touching the strings, the music palpitating, traveling from the depth of the aperture, swelling as it entered the physical space of the room. The beauty of the music made me feel alive and unstoppable.

After my decision, I went to my next class as usual. My teacher invited me to stay after class, and he played some songs. When he stopped playing, he watched me with his big brown eyes as though attempting to read my thoughts. I prepared to speak the words I had rehearsed but froze. I was afraid that he might laugh at me or just tell me I was not quite good enough to be a professional. Or maybe he would discourage me, reminding me how difficult it would be to compete with many talented musicians. But this was my only chance to make my life my own; I had to take it.

Feeling like I was jumping off a cliff, I heard myself say, "I would like to become a professional musician."

It took him a few seconds to respond, so I had time to feel how ridiculous it sounded and be prepared to run away and hide somewhere where no one would find me. My stomach tightened, my palms were sweating, and the room felt freezing. I had exposed my innermost feelings and hopes of my own free will.

The silence was deafening. I looked up, and there was a smile on my teacher's face, a delighted, approving smile that spoke volumes. I could clearly see how excited he was at the idea.

Before I could stop myself, I ran to him and wrapped my arms around him, all the while saying, "Thank you, thank you, thank you." I could not control the sobs triggered by a feeling I was unfamiliar with - a joy so pure it rang in my ears, sang in my head, and danced through my body.

When I regained control of my good manners and finally let him go, I was relieved to see that the smile was still there, illuminating his kind and sensitive face. He asked me to come back the following day and meet with the director of the *conservatoire* so they could discuss my future. I was so excited! It seemed so strange to be conspiring with two adults who were determined to support me.

The next day, the director came up with the fantastic idea that I should spend the summer at a music school run by Ida Presti and Alexandre Lagoya. All I would do there, all day long, is learn from these two stellar guitar players and practice so I would be prepared and ready to take the exam that would allow me to enroll in the *Conservatoire de Paris*, the most respected music school in France where a classical guitar curriculum had just been created. Under normal circumstances, the age limit to enter was much younger, but because this was a newly created course, the school accepted teenagers. This was a unique opportunity.

Never before had I been as happy as I was then. But something disconcerting was fighting its way to the forefront of my thoughts. What about Damien? What about Reine? What would they do when they heard about the plan? I voiced my concern to my co-conspirators, who agreed to meet my parents to encourage them to send me to music school for the summer. What could possibly go wrong?

They set up a meeting. In the following days, time passed at an excruciatingly slow pace. Then, at two o'clock on Saturday, with impeccable punctuality, my teacher and the music school Director rang the doorbell. Reine showed them into the living room, where the four adults sat down. She offered her guests a cup of coffee and a slice of cake, which they politely accepted. Inside, I was screaming, "Enough with the pleasantries! Let's get down to business!"

Finally, they broached the subject. Both my teacher and the Director spoke eloquently about me, the talented daughter, my hard work and dedication, their belief that I could make it in the music world, and the support they were willing to offer me. Although Reine was genuinely pleased, I could tell Damien was not impressed.

The Director presented them with our plan. Reine was a great fan of Ida Presti and Alexandre Lagoya, and she seemed to welcome the idea of her daughter becoming a famous musician; maybe she felt it reflected well on her, or perhaps she could finally see something valuable in me hidden from view for all these years. She clearly valued the opinion of these two professionals, who seemed serious about helping me along the way.

Damien asked a few questions but clearly did not care about the answers. No one had ever shown interest in me so far, and, in doing so, perhaps he felt they were challenging his authority and threatened his control over me. Maybe he felt he was losing ground, which made him angry.

His mind seemed already made up, it was as though he was just looking for a way to say no without his dislike of me being too apparent. However, I thought there was still a chance my mother could tip the balance in my favor.

Finally, Damien spoke as a decent, wise, reasonable man would, one who was only thinking about his daughter's 'best' interest.

"Look", he said, "Taja must study for her upcoming exam at the end of this school year and the next. She has to go to university, get a job and learn to provide for herself." He stopped for a moment.

"So, music is secondary right now, and what you suggest will only distract her from what is essential." He stopped, already looking like he had won the argument.

"But she has a chance to study with Ida Presti and Alexandre Lagoya!" my mother exclaimed as if only the names, pronounced out loud, could give rise to awe and make him reconsider.

Annoyed by his wife's remark, Damien dropped his pretense.

"You really want to let her go?" he asked, hardly containing his irritation.

"We do not know anything about this school. What if she does not study at all? You know what she is like! And it is expensive! Plus, she will be free to come and go as she pleases. God knows what could happen!"

My teacher and the director were taken aback; they had not expected Damien to pass up the chance offered to his daughter. I knew the battle was lost when they got up to leave. I was awfully embarrassed by Damien's behavior. His sense of self-importance was as infuriating as was his dismissal of their proposal. I wished I had forewarned our visitors; I had not wanted them to be exposed to that.

Damien walked them to the door and said he needed time to think. But he had already made up his mind and fooled no one. Then, with a gesture, he ushered them out.

His reaction was no surprise, but still came as a blow. I had believed - or at least hoped - that the authority of these musical experts would impress him, maybe even corner him in such a way that he just could not refuse without revealing his hostility towards me, but I was wrong.

Despite the setback, I continued to attend music classes and work with my teacher. The first time I went back after the meeting, I felt defeated. As soon as he saw me, he took me aside and said, "Taja, don't worry; we can still find a way!"

His big brown eyes revealed a passion from which there was no escape. I felt comforted and renewed. Hope swelled up inside. From then on, I was more determined than ever, practicing for hours every day until I could no longer feel my fingers. I improved in leaps and bounds. In the meantime, I stayed away from Damien as much as possible.

For the last few months, all the guitar students had been preparing for the end-of-the-year exam in early May. Guitar classes were spread over five years of study, and students of each level would play in front of four judges, who would then decide who won the competition at each level. I was in my first year, but my teacher's plan was to prepare me for the fifth-year final exam.

I had prepared three pieces I now knew by heart and was playing them beautifully, although the fourth piece by Bartok that I did not care for ended up on the back burner. When the big day came around, I was a nervous wreck. As the loudspeaker announced my name, I entered a large, empty room with only a solitary chair in the middle, a footrest, and a stand for the music sheets. In front of me, further back, was a long wooden desk resting on a platform. Four people were sitting behind it, three men and a woman looking down at me, making me feel even more nervous and intimidated.

We exchanged a few words before they invited me to start playing. I was motionless for a second, then wiping my hands and positioning the guitar on my knee, I began to play. My anxiety lasted only a few seconds; I quickly got lost in the music. I was a different person, no longer able to separate my body, hands, and fingers from my guitar; unfamiliar confidence took over, sustaining the moment.

I played the three pieces with only a short pause between each, just to position my music sheets. When I was done, I looked up at the judges and felt encouraged by the attentive expression in their eyes. One of the men spoke and asked me to proceed with the Bartok piece I had so foolishly neglected to prepare. I could have kicked myself for being so stupid. Mumbling something about not having practiced it enough, I started playing while reading the notes. I managed to salvage the situation, but reading and playing simultaneously prevented me from immersing myself in the music as I had done with the other pieces.

When I was done playing, one of the judges admired how my guitar sounded. I told him that some months ago, I had been working on extending my fingers to a distant fret unsuccessfully, and that I eventually lost my temper and took my frustration out on the instrument, hitting it with my fist. Although the guitar remained in one piece, the wood cracked along the entire length of its upper body, which must have relieved the wood's tension, effectively altering how it sounded. The judges looked amused, and the atmosphere became more casual. After asking a few more questions, they let me go.

I did not see my teacher when I left the exam room, so, I walked back home, unsure about my performance but relieved that it was over and done.

Back home, I tried to do homework, but my mind was obsessively replaying the whole encounter, trying to read the judges' faces, hoping to figure out what the verdict would be. Managing to keep calm until the results were published the following day would be impossible. The next day, I was a bundle of nerves. I needed to do something, so I went to the closet and grabbed the vacuum cleaner. Although no housework was expected of me at this time of day, I found comfort in the familiarity of it; for a few hours, I cleaned and dusted the entire apartment, vacuumed each rug, and even scrubbed the already sparkling bathtubs.

It was late afternoon when I arrived at the *conservatoire* the next day. The results were posted next to the exam room on a white, official-looking paper listing our names. I felt my heart beat faster, as I searched for my name. It was second on the list, right below another girl's name who was a fifth-year student. It took a little while before I understood that I had made second place in the fifth-year exam! I felt I had been struck by the luck fairy.

I ran down two flights of stairs to my classroom. The door was open, and a few of my fellow students were present; everyone was excited, and the room looked brighter than usual. As I walked in, my teacher turned toward me, his burning eyes so bright. "You made us proud," he said simply.

~ REFLECTIONS & INSIGHTS ~

Later, in therapy I realized that, while Madame Valcourt tormented me with physical violence, Damien exerted emotional violence. The aversion, blame and belittling instilled in me feelings of worthlessness, shame and guilt, which led me to fear being abandoned all over again. When I was removed from Madame Valcourt's home, I went to live with my mother at Damien's place. A few months later, we moved back to the old apartment that had been my home before I was sent away. There, it did not take long for me to feel that I was just tolerated rather than welcome. I became Damien's personal servant and slave. But the world never saw. I had no right to be tired and to rest, no right to suffer, not even from physical pain, let alone complain. If my head hurt, I was told that a child my age does not have headaches. I was the black sheep. *Everything* was my fault. Everything they didn't have the courage to face.

I remember the times when Damien and Reine demanded that I kiss them good night when I was done with my evening chores, before I went to bed. I hated them so much then that having to perform that evening ritual was agonizing torture. The intent to humiliate me in the way they presented a cheek while looking away from me was so unbearable that I feared I could hit them, but I obeyed, hating myself a little more each night. They wanted me to feel the power they had over me, and my humiliation would drive that message home.

The way they treated me got under my skin, sneaked into my cells, and settled there for life. It deformed me so much that I did not know who I was anymore. There wasn't a home for me, no safe place, no safe person ... I was ugly and inspired revulsion. That's how he looked at me. And with time, I started to believe him. I accepted that I was nothing, I deserved nothing.

But my music teacher and the Director were kind, gentle, and supportive. Their eyes on me contradicted Damien's. They were warm and they believed in me, they thought I had talent, that I was special. They had gone out of their way to help me pursue a musical career. I was able to accept their friendship and their generosity wholeheartedly, and it changed me. I began to believe that I did deserve and that there was good in me, that I, too, had something worthwhile to offer, and that there was a way to escape the ever-present condemnation in Damien's eyes.

CHAPTER XVI

The Lifeline Breaks

SEPTEMBER came around. It was time to go back to school for my last year before the "*baccalauréat*." This exam was the only way to enter university and the Conservatoire de Paris, so to pursue a musical career, I had to pass.

September also meant the reopening of the conservatoire. I was thrilled to see my teacher again and return to my twice-weekly classes after I practiced non-stop that summer.

As the school year started, my stepfather, busy with his thriving business, paid less attention to what was happening at home. By then, my parents employed maids who did most of the work I had been doing for years. They never lasted very long; I am not sure why. I do remember that the idea that someone would be working for me the way I had worked for my stepfather made me feel very uncomfortable. I continued to clean my room, shine my shoes, and take care of my stuff so no one else would have to.

Although I had little housework to do, I did not have a moment of inactivity; I was either practicing my instrument or reading my schoolbooks until the letters began to dance before my eyes. When we went away for the weekend to Damien's sister's house in Fontainebleau, I would head for the basement as soon as we arrived and stay down there to play music and study the entire weekend, only making rare appearances when it was time to set the table, eat, clean or go for a walk in the woods. As much as I loved the forest, I used to hate those snail-paced walks with the Bivas "family" and the mundane conversations that drowned the sounds and silences of nature.

It must have been late February when the unfathomable happened. I was coming back from music class after a particularly wonderful time. I had stayed after class as I often did. We had played duets, and then I had asked my teacher to play a cherished piece by Villa-Lobos. Sitting in that familiar room full of memories, I had felt the world was mine. When I left that evening, I was singing out loud on my way back home. The streets were empty, and I took my time. I wanted to savor the joy. I did not want the feeling to stop; I did not want to return to my desolate life.

I THE INVISIBLE SELF

It was a few minutes past eight o'clock when I let myself into our apartment, I could hear my parents in the dining room, but I went straight to my room, deposited my guitar on my bed, took my coat off, stopped by the door for a second, took a deep breath before heading for in the dining room.

As I entered the room, I immediately knew I was in trouble. Reine sat at the dinner table, but Damien stood in the middle of the room. His eyes were cold, unforgiving. I had seen that look so many times before. His voice betrayed the barely contained indignation of an insulted man.

"It is past eight o'clock," he said calmly, the perfectly filed nail of his left index finger tapping the watch on his right wrist.

"You know that we eat at eight o'clock in this house! It's your job to set the table! Where were you?" It was a question, but I knew he was not interested in my answer, so I remained quiet.

"Where were you?" he repeated, hoping to discomfort me.

"I was in music class," I replied wearily, as he was perfectly aware of my whereabouts.

"What makes you think that you can show up late? Do you expect to just sit down to dinner and be served?"

"No, no! I just stayed a little longer, just this once," I cried out. I felt a tightening in my throat, but I did not want to break down in front of him. I could not bear to give him the satisfaction that transpired in his entire demeanor. It would puff him up, make him look taller and proud.

"Oh, really? Just *a little* longer! Well, I have news for you. As long as you live under my roof, you do as I say, you follow my rules, and if you don't, the door is wide open." He extended his arm in the direction of the front door.

"It won't happen again," I promised.

"No, it won't! Because you are done with your guitar classes. You're not going back, ever!"

I froze. I could not believe my ears. Surely, he was just kidding; this was not for real. I looked at Reine, who did not say a word. Sitting down to have dinner with them would have required superhuman effort, so I ran to my room and slammed the door behind me. I sat on my bed and looked at my guitar. I just could not believe it was the end.

I lay down with my clothes on. I needed to calm down, but my heart was beating fast. The thoughts in my head were flying by quickly. Hate, sadness, and despair overtook me. I felt I was at war, and this enemy of mine had taken the last thing he could possibly take from me. I was becoming dangerously aware that now I had power, the power that those with nothing left to lose have. That power is what leads to revolutions.

I looked out the large bay window at the city lights. There was a world out there, a whole world away from this place, and soon, I would escape, flee, and never look back. Of course, I had been naïve to imagine that I could fight a war all by myself. What had I expected to accomplish all alone?

Life went on as if nothing had happened. I kept preparing for the *baccalauréat* I needed to pass to enter university. I barely spoke to Reine or Damien; I answered when spoken to, but that was the extent of our communication. I went to school, got back, took care of the household chores, sat down to eat, cleaned up, and retired to my room to study. At school, I did not tell my friends anything, and they knew little about me anyhow. I did not know how to look for support and empathy.

Little by little, I came to worry I would not pass my exam. I was going to take a literary *baccalauréat*, which made Latin, French, Philosophy, and History the most important subjects of my written exam. But something inside triggered serious doubts about my ability to succeed, which worsened as time passed. The exam at the end of the year hovered over me like a huge dark cloud. Day by day, it was turning darker, and soon, there seemed to be nothing else; it suffocated me. I wanted to run away from it, but there was nowhere to go.

I made one last attempt; I went to see the social worker at our school. It was difficult to speak at first, but she was kind and understanding. She helped me open up a little. With her tactful questions guiding me, I spoke of Damien and Reine and how I felt like their prisoner.

After our consultation, she invited my parents to a meet with her at my school. I had hoped that she would convey her concerns for my wellbeing and that they would respect her professional authority enough to listen to some of her suggestions. But my hopes melted like ice in the sun when I saw the look on my parents' faces as they came home. They were furious, both of them.

"What have you been telling this woman about us?! Do you have any idea of what you made us look like? Did you think for one minute before you decided to go and tell tales to her? Are you happy now?!"

My needs did not exist, and neither did my grief. I was trying to save myself, but they could not see that. They were the victimized parents. I was beginning to understand that there would never be a way out for me. I felt I could not keep on struggling anymore. I finally understood how useless it all was.

*

My 18th birthday was coming up. I decided it would be the day I would end my life. I thought this was the only way out. Late in the evening I went to my mother's medicine cabinet and swallowed pills without even knowing what they were. Then back in my room, too devastated to even cry, I just lay there and fell asleep.

Early the following morning, despite all the pills, I woke up. My bladder was burning. I heard my mother busy in another room, and for a minute, I wished I could run to her, throw myself into her arms and tell her what I had done. But then, I remembered her coldness, and the impulse died down as quickly as it had emerged.

I waited until I could not hear her voice anymore, quietly cracked my door open, and once I was sure no one was around, I ran to the medicine cabinet and swallowed the contents of another bottle of pills my mother used for headaches. I had a romantic idea of death; I considered suicide an act of courage. Again, I fell asleep.

Later that morning, as I was still in bed, halfway between consciousness and sleep, my mother walked into my room. It was the first time I had ever stayed in bed that late, especially on a school day. She asked me to get up and ready, but I did not respond. Her tone climbed quickly to a screech, but I ignored her. She screamed angrily and walked out of my room, slamming the door shut behind her with such violence that the three tiny paintings of my favorite Parisian *Poulbots* crashed to the floor.

I felt relief; I was escaping, going to a place where they could no longer hurt me, belittle me, abuse me. I longed to be set free and never again be afraid, ashamed, and exhausted. I cried myself to sleep.

Later that day, when I did not appear at dinner, Reine and Damien finally decided that something was wrong. I was told later they had entered my room, found me unconscious, and attempted to wake me. I don't remember much, only the instant when my stepfather slapped me. But I was not angry at him, there was fear in his voice, faint and distant as he attempted to bring me back to consciousness.

I felt movement around me, but in my world, darkness had set in. Pressure was applied to my left foot, and I heard what sounded like rushed whispers, "There is no reaction," "Nothing," and "Oh no, so young." Then nothing ...

I was in a coma for three days. When I woke up, I was floating in white, cotton clouds. At first, I could not see anything at all. Little by little, my eyes began to focus, and the first thing I noticed was my mother's face, pain showing in her eyes. I could not remember having seen such a concerned expression on her face. Her silhouette was still surrounded by clouds when I heard myself ask:

"Where is Papa?" Damien was next to her, a few inches further away but I could not see him until my depth of field slowly returned. Then the room came into focus. He did not look mean. But it was my real father I was asking for.

During my stay, I had a few sessions with a psychiatrist. He was cold and impersonal, as were his questions. I felt uncomfortable in his dark and cramped office and refused to tell him anything about myself. He was clearly annoyed, but I did not care.

It was concluded that my suicide attempt was due to George, my boyfriend at the time, breaking up with me. I had not been in love with George, and I felt sorry that he was made responsible when he had nothing to do with it. I felt it was a heavy burden to put on an eighteen-year-old boy. My mother never acknowledged my stepfather's role, and hers, in my "emotional breakdown." Couldn't she grasp that they had trampled my hopes and dreams one too many times?

I remained in the hospital for a few more days, then was discharged and sent back home where I stayed until the end of the school year. For the time being, Damien was not tormenting me.

Studying did not seem to matter anymore. I spent a lot of time doing nothing, and it felt strange in a good way. School friends were allowed to come and visit or pick me up. We took slow walks in the neighborhood or sat on benches savoring the warm and sunny essence of spring afternoons. Spring soon turned into early summer, bringing back a sense of warmth, ease, and hope despite what had happened.

Not too long after I returned home from the hospital, my mother had a nervous breakdown and spent the next few weeks in a private clinic in Paris. I went to visit her a couple of times but could not stay for too long. Her despair was too much, I could not listen to her words, and I couldn't bear her tears. I felt exhausted and emotionally blunted when I was around her.

Meanwhile, the time came to take the *baccalauréat*. I did not feel there was any point in trying but Damien insisted that I try regardless of the results. He even went as far as driving me each day to the Parisian lycée where the exam was taking place. Expecting to fail, I took the written exam, then the oral tests in Latin, French, English, and Philosophy.

When it was all over, I remember walking across the big hall toward the exit while the results were read out loud by someone with a microphone. There seemed no point in my waiting. Just as I was about to step out, I heard my name. I was sure I was mistaken but when I checked the written list plastered on the wall, to my astonishment, I saw that I had passed.

CHAPTER XVII

Summer In Israel

IT WAS in Israel, at Ramat Hakovesh, that I met André for the first time. Little did I know that my life was about to change forever.

After my suicide attempt, Reine thought that a change of scenery would be good for me. Jacqueline was leaving with a group of young people for Israel that summer, and Reine decided to send me there too. Damien wanted me to work that summer to cover the cost of my hospital bills, but for once his opinion didn't count. The school psychologist, my mother, and my grandmother protested and brushed his demand aside.

We sailed the Mediterranean and landed in Athens for a day. I was reading the *Colossus of Maroussi* by Henry Miller at the time. I had picked that book off the shelves of a bookstore not knowing what it was about. But what a choice it turned out to be! The way the author captured the essence of Greece, and the Greek people was thrilling.

With my grandmother's tales echoing in my ears, I imagined wandering along the streets of Thessaloniki, sitting at the long tables where neighborhood families had gathered, drinking cold, fruity wine, tasting divine dishes my grandmother still cooked. There were olive trees all around. Their ripe, crunchy fruits soaked in red vinegar and herbs tasted heavenly. I remember fondly Sarina's thick rolling "*r, s*" that never seemed to end when she had explained with uncontained excitement that these were "des Kalamatas d'*o*rigine!!" She received them from Greece, plump and ripe, and she lovingly prepared them in her tiny kitchen just as she had been taught when she was a young girl.

The sun was shining when Athens came into view. Up high above the city where stood the Acropolis, the Parthenon was breathtaking. Mesmerized by the beauty, the history of the century's old stones, I imagine traveling back in time to ancient Greece, lost for words to describe something one can only feel, absorb, time layered over time for thousands of years. I was intimidated but captivated. I felt the power of history when the thread of generations past comes together. Then, someone called my name and I looked away.

When we docked, I met with members of grandmother's family, and close friends she had known since childhood. I was not sure how we were related exactly but it was like meeting long-lost friends; we hugged and ate and drank and hugged again. They were so happy to meet me, their joyful mood and their warmth made me feel at home. They had never met me before, but there was no doubt I was family to them.

We rejoined our ship that departed before sundown, and I sobbed quietly as I watched the Parthenon lit by a late afternoon golden light, slowly being left behind. I did not want to leave, and promised myself I would return and live there someday.

A day later, we landed in Haifa. We waited while our passports were checked. Behind a metal fence, Israeli people were waiting to greet disembarking travelers. A commotion made me look up and I saw people running to the crowd gathered on the other side. There were screams, and there were tears, and there were touching fingers, the only body part that could pass through the wire mesh, touching like they would never ever let go. It evoked something in me I could not remember. I felt there was such deep sorrow under the joy and happiness of their homecoming. Later, I was told that these men and women were family and friends who had lost each other during the war. Some had escaped the Nazis and settled in Israel, others had been deported. For some, it took years of searching to find their loved ones. What I was witnessing was their reunion after all these years.

In just a few days, I had reconnected with my Greek roots and then my Jewish roots. Finally, I felt I was unconditionally accepted without having to do anything other than simply being myself. It was like being where my DNA had determined I belonged.

From Haifa, a bus took us to the kibbutz, Ramat Hakovesh. There, we were shown to the barracks. The "room" was minuscule, a place to sleep with bunk beds on each side that I shared with Jacqueline and a couple of other girls in our group.

We used to get a wake-up knock on our door at around 4 a.m. I would stumble outside, follow the others, pour coffee in a beat-up metal mug, and climb onto the bed of one of the army trucks that drove us to a pear orchard a few miles away. It was still dark and cold, but we wore army shorts, tees, shirts, and hats. The sun would rise in a couple of hours, and the temperature would climb high. We usually worked until 7:30 a.m. and then got a break. Everyone sat around long wooden tables for breakfast. Half an hour later, we would return to our row of trees and pick pears until it seemed like all the ripe ones had been harvested. Then we would climb down, grab our ladder, and move further down the line of planted trees. We would pass friendly sunburnt faces appearing through the thick leafy branches and look for a new tree to harvest.

It was just another one of those sunny mornings. I was perched on top of a tree, picking pears, occasionally eating one too ripe to be transported. They were sweet as candy. I was unaware that someone had climbed up the other side of my tree. Suddenly, a nicely tanned face and a big friendly smile broke through the branches.

"Hi," he said. "My name is André. What's yours?"

"Taja," I replied and carried on working.

"Where are you from, Taja?"

"Paris," I replied. "The 12th arrondissement."

"No way!" He seemed incredulous. "That's where I live too!"

I stopped for a moment and looked at him. I was sure he was just making it up, having fun at my expense, but he seemed genuinely surprised. He was good-looking. His confidence was intimidating but I liked him. We kept working, carrying our ladders from one tree to the next. He would lean his ladder close to the trunk and climb up high, and I would do the same on the opposite side. We moved from tree to tree and met across the upper branches while picking pears, but we were much more interested in each other than in the work at hand. We finished our shift early in the afternoon. He told me later that our meeting had not been accidental. He had seen me for the first time at breakfast that morning, and when I went back to work, he had grabbed his ladder and run down the sandy path to catch up with me.

Late that afternoon, he came by and asked if I'd like to join him for a walk after dinner. I accepted and met him later in what we called the garden, even though it was not much of a garden, more like a sandy desert patch. The sky was dark, and the stars were brilliant, so close I felt I could touch them if I just reached up. A few people passed us on their way to their barracks. André and I walked silently for a while, then sat down on the swings.

"Why did you choose to come to Israel for the summer?" André asked me.

I remained quiet for a moment. "I did not choose; it was kind of decided for me."

"What do you mean?" he asked.

I was unsure how much I was willing to tell him. "Well, I was not okay last year ... I had problems with my family, and they sent me here to ... recover.

"Recover? From what?" he asked.

I got up from the swing and started walking slowly and quietly in circles. Finally, I whispered, "I tried to kill myself." He was quiet, but his eyes questioned for more. So, I went on.

"I felt I had nothing to live for ... it was like being in jail, trapped. I thought I could never escape. I'm still not sure I have. I'm just far away, that's all." I stopped, out of breath, shocked by all the words that had come out all at once.

He looked at me for the longest time with knowing eyes, wise beyond his years, and said almost matter-of-factly, "That was brave and stupid; I'm glad you're here."

I was not exactly sure what he had meant, but I knew it did not come from a place of meanness or judgment; he was just expressing his thought out loud.

Why could I connect with this cool guy so easily? Was it the heat? Was it that I could smell the wonderful sunny scent of his skin? Was it his longish black hair, his intelligent hazel eyes? I inched closer to him. He looked up, then he kissed me softly. His lips felt like silk against mine.

He got up from the swing, wrapped his arms around me, and just held me tight. We touched, shy and hungry all at once, lost in the delight of intimate discovery.

I had never felt so close to another living being. I thought it would be okay if my life was to end right there and then. It would be a good time to die. Passion swept over us like an irresistible wave bringing us together like the tide that sweeps you away and brings you back closer, and there is not a thing you can do to resist its force. We spent the night walking as far as we could in the desert dunes, oblivious of lurking dangers, just drinking the nectar of life as if it was our last night on earth. Later, we sat on top of a sand dune, looking at the dark horizon until it turned from black to a deep blue, the color of the sky in one of my favorite Magritte paintings. We just sat there together in absolute silence. I was back on earth and among the living, back from the loneliest voyage that had just ended with André's appearance.

When André left the kibbutz that summer, I wondered if I would ever see him again. At the time, I did not understand how unique he was, or how deeply his leaving had affected me. But I soon discovered that whiskey freed me from the sadness that was now tormenting me. In the evenings, I ended up at the kibbutz's night club dancing late into the night, drinking the golden brew with abandon. It took away the anguish of feeling inadequate and cast my inhibitions to the wind.

As the end of our stay in Ramat Hakovesh approached, free to do as we pleased, Jacqueline and I decided to hitchhike our way down south to Eilat.

*

We arrived in Beersheba after sundown and rented a room for the night at a youth hostel not far from the Camel Market. In the early hours as the sun rose, we got up wondering how we would manage a 230-plus-kilometer trip across the Negev. We walked until a market came into view. It was set in a big open space with all sorts of vendors selling everything from fruits and vegetables to spices and nuts. Intermingled Bedouins, Jews and Arabs walked or sat around surrounded by camels, goats and donkeys that seemed to be part of the family. Colorful, decorated fabrics were spread on the ground; meats were covered with flies.

There were army trucks and soldiers everywhere. One of them gestured for us to approach. We pointed south and asked, "Eilat?" He gestured again, inviting us to climb up. We sat there with a group of heavily armed soldiers. They could not have been much older than us.

They welcomed us with bright smiles, and, if not for their weapons, they looked harmless. The truck soon departed and began its slow bumpy crossing. There were no roads, just golden sand dunes and flats as far as the eye could see.

Unexpectedly, the truck stopped and dropped us off, as it prepared to turn inland to an invisible destination. Jordanian soldiers were lying in the sand at the top of high dunes that marked the border between the two enemy countries, their machine guns pointed at us. Jacqueline and I had no idea how far we had gone. We waited, hoping a car would soon pick us up and drive us down to our destination.

As time went by, the sun climbed high in the sky, bleaching the golden sand and deep blue of the early morning sky. The heat was beating down on us mercilessly. We looked for shade but there was none. We sat down and waited while our arms, legs, and faces turned to deeper shades by the minute.

I was drifting off to sleep when I heard a hissing sound that couldn't be mistaken. I looked sideways to Jaqueline, our eyes met, and we sprang up like uncorked genies. Without looking back, we sprinted to the road that could only be guessed at by the remaining tire threads imprinted in the sand. I later learned that we had had a close encounter with a Saharan sand viper, a small venomous snake that lives in sand dunes by day and hides under bushes buried in the sand. We had picked just the right spot!

A vehicle approached in a cloud of dust. Thankfully, the old and rusty Beetle stopped, and a couple of bearded American hippies picked us up. We chatted for a few minutes, then fell asleep on the back seat.

In Eilat, they dropped us off. We thanked them and waved as they shouted goodbye. That's when we caught sight of each other, shocked by the great dark circles beneath our sunken eyes. We were severely dehydrated and sunburned! Our crossing of the desert felt like an otherworldly interlude. We were lucky to be alive.

The main street of Eilat was just a dusty road lined with small buildings, clothing shops and an impressive number of coffee shops. We walked the length of it, asking for "*mitz escholius*" - grapefruit juice - in each bar, gulping down bottle after bottle of the divine ice-cold juice, sweet with a tangy bitter aftertaste until our thirst was quenched.

Later, as the sun descended behind the mountains, we sat on a low stone wall, sipping ice-cold coffee. I was drawn to the flickering lights of Aqaba, on the Jordan side of border. In the distance, the ancient town looked magical, its old golden stone buildings filled with hidden secrets. I remembered that magnificent scene in the film *Lawrence of Arabia* when Lawrence attacks Aqaba, his horsemen galloping down from the desert behind, reaching the gorgeous cerulean sea.

On a whim, we decided to walk across the Jordan border ignoring the barbed wire and rusty signs in Arabic and English that prohibited access to this war zone that was crawling with militia and snipers. We headed towards Aqaba when without warning, and out of nowhere, we were surrounded by a small group of soldiers, their machine guns pointed at us. Looking at us suspiciously, they shouted something incomprehensible. We stood there, blinking in the bright light shining on us. An older man who seemed to be in charge spoke in broken English. We pretended to be lost. It was obvious he did not believe us. But after exchanging a few words between themselves, the soldiers walked us back to the border and gestured for us to "get lost."

~ REFLECTIONS & INSIGHTS ~

The traumas I had repressed in early life left me oblivious of these present dangers.

I had often wondered what had led me to even contemplate such reckless adventures, and what had been driving me to endanger my life so frequently? Years later, I discovered that my counter-phobic behaviors were a way to avoid remembering the dangers of the past. They kept the terror of my abusive childhood out of consciousness.

And it worked for a while.

*

Our time in Israel had come to an end. We returned to Haifa to board the ship that would take us back to Italy. After depositing my backpack in our cabin, I left Jacqueline and climbed back on deck to savor the brightness of the day, the shimmering ripples of the water, and the warmth of the breeze caressing my skin. I had been standing there for a while, lost in contemplation and inner thoughts of freedom. Suddenly, I sensed a presence behind me. I turned around, and I just saw him standing there. André! He was tall, dark, and his unbuttoned white shirt was dancing in the breeze. That image burnt into my brain cells for eternity. He moved closer and wrapped his arms around me, his fragrance spicy and salty and sweet all at once. I was home again.

"What are you doing here?" he asked with a twinkle in his eye.

"What are *you* doing here?" I replied smiling.

"Our ship sank ... a few weeks back ..."

I did not let him finish, "You can't be serious!!"

But he did look serious. In fact, I found out later that the ship had been the *Andromachi*, damaged and set afire by Israeli shelling earlier that summer.

It was so very strange. I could not help but wonder if it was a random incident, or destiny perhaps that had brought us together a second time.

Unfortunately, by then, the pain of early my childhood abandonment had been unearthed and could no longer be restrained. The thought of going back to my old life was unbearable. It drove me to drink more and more, seeking oblivion. The days passed in a blur and, as we got closer to Italy, where we would disembark and catch a train back to Paris, the fear of losing André became intolerable.

He never gave up on me and was by my side most of the time. I remember him sitting beside me on the tiled shower floor, cold water running down on us both as he attempted to sober me up after I had had a few drinks too many.

I barely remember the ride to Paris. As the train finally came to a halt, the flow of descending travelers intermingled with the crowds gathered at Gare de Lyon. Excitement was in the air. In the ensuing confusion, somehow, André vanished. We never had a chance to say goodbye. I had no idea whether his disappearance had been accidental or intentional.

LEAVING HOME

After I got back home from Israel, I realized that there was a better life waiting for me out there, a world of possibilities that Damien had made unreachable for me, but now it was different.

Since I was 12 years old, as I left our apartment to go to school in the early mornings, my grandmother had been waiting for me in her kitchen next door, hot coffee and chicory brewing, toasted bread and butter set on the table. We did not have much time but during these few minutes, I would confide in her. I would tell her about Damien's overwhelming demands and would not stop dreaming out loud about escaping from my miserable existence.

And time after time, she would beg me to hang on, to wait until I was 18. She would describe an exciting life of independence, away from him, a promise of freedom that would only be possible after I finished high school, when the time would come for me to go to university.

And now, I was back home, I had finished high school. My time had come!

I wanted to study medicine and had planned to have my own room close to campus. But my stepfather had other plans for me. If I wanted to study, I would have to live with them indefinitely.

This came as no surprise and a showdown with Damien had been inevitable - it was a matter of *when* not *if.*

"If you leave this house, I'll cut you off! And don't count on me to cover the cost of your education. You make your choice, and you live with it!"

It was a threat I had heard many times before, but now I had had enough. My eyes locked into his. The blackmail gave rise to rage; I felt it erupting inside, years of unexpressed rage. I showed nothing and said nothing. But I knew there was no coming back from that.

I turned away, went to my room, and slammed the door shut behind me. I grabbed my backpack, threw a few clothes in it, and walked out of my room. Bewildered by my resolve, I turned to my mother, who had witnessed the scene without a word.

"Where are my savings?" I asked.

"It's gone; the account is closed" Reine replied coldly.

All the little coins and bills I had received for good behavior, school accomplishments, and birthdays had vanished. Any remnant of warmth toward my mother was instantly evaporated instantly. And I walked out ...

Once outside, I paused for a moment. What I had done took my breath away. Then, heading for the main street, I saw the small suburban station in the distance where I used to take a train to my high school in Le Raincy. I would meet my friends there; we would climb the metal steps and let the train take us to school, wishing we could skip class and run away somewhere, anywhere.

This time, I was alone and going in the opposite direction, towards Paris. Around me, everything was gray ... the afternoon sky, the buildings, the curbs. A few cars drove by; the street was otherwise deserted. It was about four o'clock, and people were not back from work just yet.

Countless emotions were coming up. They were too loud, all jumbled up like voices at a cocktail party, making it difficult to separate one feeling from another.

After losing one battle after another, finally, I triumphed and set myself free. I had turned my back on a meaningless life lived in terror under Damien's regime. I had no idea where I was going to stay, and I had no idea what tomorrow would bring. I only had 100 francs in my pocket and a small suitcase with jeans, sweaters, some of my favorite books, all of it thrown in in a hurry and without much thought.

I knew one thing with absolute certainty: I was never going back.

CHAPTER XVIII

A Brave New Life

THE SOCIAL UPHEAVAL of the 1960s and early 1970s was a perfect backdrop for a life on the edge.

I found myself on the street, homeless, penniless, with the northern European winter looming. I had no plan, no goal, and no destination. It felt like basic survival from one day to the next. Now and then, I found odd jobs. When money ran out, I spent the night outside. When I had enough money, I rented a room for the night in a hotel in the *Quartier Latin*. I was very fond of the kind woman who ran the place. She always brought me breakfast, free of charge. I never forgot the aroma of the freshly brewed coffee as I savored the delicious hot croissants she never failed to add to the tray, crusty on the outside, melting on the inside, a delight for the tastebuds.

At nightfall, I would climb up the carpeted stairs, turn the heavy key in the lock and enter my room. I remember the sense of well-being as I slipped between the clean white sheets and laid my head on the soft pillows for the night. I would soon fall asleep, safe and warm, until her soft knock on my door in the early hours.

On other nights, I curled up on a bench in Bois de Vincennes by the edge of the dark and shiny lake, which reflected nothing more than the dim glow of streetlamps. It was flat and lifeless at times, then shivering when gusts of a cold winter wind rippled its black surface. It seemed like an appropriate place to be, a match to the darkness of the thoughts running through my head. I could still feel the heat of the tears rolling down my cheeks, a remnant of my rage, leaving only a dry streak of saltiness on my lips. I believe this lifelong ability to cry out my distress saved my sanity.

The stinging chill of the night would find its way all too easily under the layers of clothing and soon enough under my skin. Fighting the weather was useless; before long, my muscles would turn to stone. I would feel my brain slow down as if my blood had turned solid, my cells had turned to ice, my very thoughts frozen. Thus, mercifully anesthetized, I would doze off. And then, under my eyelids shut tight, I would begin to detect the rising light of a new gray day.

*

I met Elias in a nightclub where I would take refuge when I had nowhere else to spend the night and just enough money in my pocket to buy the entry ticket. I was attempting to read *Crime and Punishment* by Fyodor Dostoevsky, who I had discovered in high school, where I had chosen Russian as my second language. Elias sat at my table, introduced himself and offered me a drink. Although the place was not crowded, the music was too loud to carry out a conversation, so he said: "How about we get out of here?"

"And go where?" I asked.

"My place? It's quiet, we can talk. I make a killer Turkish coffee too." He saw my hesitation and asked: "Where do you live?"

I could not say, "nowhere," but I thought he had guessed. I was about to refuse when I realized that I felt safe in his presence; there was nothing about him that set off red flags in me. His looks and demeanor reminded me of a young Palestinian writer I had met briefly in Akko, Israel, and whose company I had enjoyed so much. I took in Elias's nice face, curly black hair, dark skin, and warm brown eyes and felt comfortable enough to accept his invitation.

His place was close by, a long-term rental in a hotel next to the Sorbonne, where he was a student. He was quiet while preparing coffee and then sat next to me on the couch. We did not talk much. He saw I was exhausted and invited me to spend the night on his couch. I did not think twice and accepted. Elias pulled a huge T-shirt from a bottom drawer and showed me to the bathroom shared by the hotel residents, one floor up. Taking a hot bath felt like the ultimate luxury. The fresh lavender scent of the soap transported me back in time. When I went back to the room, I lay down on the couch, wrapped myself in a blanket and fell asleep before my head hit the pillow.

The next morning, I woke up to find a note pinned next to my pillow: "Stay the day and rest, I'll be back this afternoon!" I wondered why he was so generously offering me his hospitality. But I did not care and went back to sleep until he showed up by nightfall.

Elias and I spent the next couple of months together. At first it felt like a comfortable friendship, then we grew closer and became lovers. We took long subway rides and visited Paris, always at night. When the subway stations closed, we walked for hours back to the hotel through the deserted streets. Touches of light from the old-fashioned, quaint, streetlamps interspersing the darkness sometimes made me feel like I had stepped into a painting from another era.

Not long after we first met, Elias asked if I wanted to stop working for a while; he said he had enough money to support us both, and that we would have more time together. I was only too happy to let go of the underpaid jobs I would get at the time. The lazy mornings I spent curled up in bed, not having to face the cold winter mornings felt like a life of pure luxury.

It was during that time that he introduced me to hashish. I had no idea where he was getting his supply, but he obviously had contacts and never ran out. I learned to roll my own joints and smoked only now and then at first. It felt like we lived each day as if it was our last, the future was just tomorrow. At the time, I never had bad reactions when I smoked, and I think it was because I felt safe in our hotel room, with no strangers around.

*

Soon, our bliss came to an end. Elias' mother was an Arabic Lebanese woman who married a high-profile politician from France.

When the father learned from acquaintances that his son was dating a Jewish girl, he flew to Paris to bring Elias back to Beirut. Elias promised he would come back the day he turned 21, which was only a few months away.

Father and son left like thieves in the night, leaving me alone with a 100-franc bill on the night table. For several days, I had felt I knew how the story would unfold and how it would end. Everything happened as I had foreseen and dreaded. And now he was gone.

Curled up on the big, battered bed, I was emptied, exhausted, my eyes still swollen with tears, my heart filled with grief. For a while, I just stared into nothingness like a wounded animal resigned to the trap. Then, my gaze focused once more on the hotel room and the familiar objects that had formed our world - my world with Elias, now shattered.

I lay on the bed and dreamed about becoming an amnesiac. How wonderful it would be to get a new start in life with no more destructive memories!

As the night was approaching, I was afraid that I was going to disappear if I did not move. I thought I might go for a walk or maybe have a drink at a café, anything rather than stay in my room where memories assaulted me mercilessly. I needed some distraction.

I sat up and looked around. There was nothing more than a sink with two faucets, one for hot and one for cold, a mirror, and a large metal bucket I had bought a while back. I placed the bucket in front of the small sink and let my clothes slide to the floor. The sensation of the lukewarm water running down my skin felt like it was washing away the pain. I shampooed my hair, rinsed it time and again, until I felt refreshed enough. I stepped out onto a towel on the floor and dried the water with another. I made up my eyes, powdered my nose, put my jeans and a favorite old sweater on, grabbed my jacket, and left.

Although it was evening now, there was a delicious aroma of coffee and warm bread floating in the air in the hotel lobby. As I stepped outside, the street's familiar sounds startled me after the long hours of silence spent in the room alone. The streets were packed with people moving fast in every direction. Not sure what to do or where to go, I started down the boulevard, in slow motion while crowds rushed all around me. I felt disconnected from the world, the sounds were muffled, it felt unreal. The turmoil inside separated me from everyone; my despair was so deep it could not be communicated.

I kept walking and walking, glancing at the cafes and the stores all lit up, without focus. I must have walked up and down the boulevard for hours when I noticed the metro station right in front of me. I began to walk down the stairs leading to the subway green entrance doors that kept popping open as people rushed in and out. I could feel the warmth and breathed in the air, filled with the smell of hot metal. I could hear the screeching sounds of the subway wheels. I went all the way down to the platform, stood there for a while, then sat down, looking at the white tiles on the walls. The station's name, "Saint-Michel," was written in large blue letters made up of tiles too. The trains came and went, green cars for second class and red for first class.

I did not know how long I had sat there. I felt I was waiting for something ... or someone. Finally, I stood up and started walking back toward the exit. People were running up and down the stairs in a rush to get wherever they were going. It was strange how so many people could be in such close proximity and yet, never make eye contact, never talk, never interact.   was a place where people's paths crossed, they bumped into each other, but everyone behaved as if no one else was there, as if all these other beings were invisible, and in a way, they were.

I looked up at the people rushing down, and that was when our eyes met. There was instant recognition as André smiled at me with an expression of incredulity on his no longer tanned face.

"I can't believe this!" he exclaimed. "What on earth are you doing here?"

"I live here," I replied. "I left home."

He looked genuinely happy to see me. "Listen, I have to go to my parents for dinner; I promised I would be there, so I can't miss it," he said. "But can I meet you after dinner? I would really like to see you and catch up.   Can I come to your place at, say, eleven?"

I nodded and quickly scribbled my address on a piece of paper.

Intrigued, he asked, "You live in a hotel?"

"Only for a few more days," I replied.

He had to run, as he was already late for dinner. I stepped onto the sidewalk at the bottom of Boulevard Saint-Michel, driven by renewed energy and a tiny little bit of joy trying to come to the surface, breaking through my sorrow.

Everything I had been feeling before my encounter with André faded. As I walked up the boulevard, I felt connected to the world again. I could now hear the sounds, see the lights, enjoy watching the crowds of strangers; I had regained my focus and felt alive.

I took my time walking back to the hotel. I was recalling the details of our encounter, savoring the moment, and anticipating the time he would knock at my door. I knew – or hoped – we would spend the night together. Then I was struck by the strange contrast between the grief and despair of the last few days, and the joy I felt now. I could sense the possibility of a new beginning; even if André never showed up, I had escaped the despair of the previous days.

Back in my hotel room, I began to clean up the mess, emptied the bucket of soapy water, washed cups and spoons, folded towels and clothes strewn on the floor. Then I stood in the middle of the room, inspecting everything with a critical eye. It was good enough.

While I was waiting, I went to the mirror a few times to retouch my makeup; I wanted to look irresistible to him. This wasn't easy for me as I had never felt irresistible; I even had a hard time feeling pretty at all.

As I was growing restless, I lay down on the bed, staring at the ceiling; then I grabbed a book, read a couple of lines, but the words got blurry, and soon I fell asleep.

There was a gentle knock at the door. I bolted up, ran to the mirror for a last glance, then went to the door to open it. Like in a dream, he was standing tall, his hands on the casing above the door, his silky black hair falling on his shoulders. A smile curled up the corners of his mouth, his brown eyes were burning with a passion for life, just the way I remembered him. I invited him in.

He did not look around for a moment, he was laser-focused on me, which made me a bit uneasy. I wished I knew what was going through his mind.

"You have changed," he finally said. "You look..." he hesitated, searching for the right words. "You look like you've ... grown. Back in Israel, you looked like a girl. You're even more beautiful now. It's the expression in your eyes that struck me when we met earlier."

"Thank you," I said, wondering what he could see in my eyes. Was I so transparent to him? I took a deep breath. I was always worried when people spoke about my looks, but André had always been someone who seemed to look beyond what just met the eye. I had sensed that about him from the very first time we had met.

I offered to make coffee, and he accepted. He dropped his long coat on the back of a chair, grabbed a pack of Gitanes and matches from his pocket, and settled down comfortably on the bed, his back leaning against the wall behind him, legs crossed. I handed him a cup of black coffee then sat down on the bed in the same position at a ninety-degree angle, our feet almost touching. I turned my head slightly and looked at him.

"How come you left home? What happened when you returned from Israel?" he asked.

I began a sentence but stopped. The words were stuck in my throat. I needed help to confide in another human being. I turned away and reached out for the side table drawer where the hashish Elias had left behind was hidden. I offered André a joint, and he nodded, so I mixed some hashish with tobacco, rolled it up, and lit it. I inhaled deeply, let out just a bit of smoke, and handed him the joint. We sat there in silence enjoying the moment.

What I loved about hash was how it removed my inhibitions. It made me feel free and exalted, my tongue untied, my movements were fluid. I was free to be in the moment without worries about being judged or getting hurt. Hash helped me stop the critical inner voices that seemed to crawl along sinuous pathways and invade my head.

I had never felt as attracted to anyone as I was to André. It was something way beyond his good looks and his undeniable charm. I trusted him completely, without reservation, and that was something I did not have much practice at. He was a stranger, and yet, I knew him. It was troubling, in a good way, but troubling, nonetheless.

We spoke well into the night. At one point, we looked at each other without holding back. I leaned toward him, and we kissed; it was the same kiss I remembered - soft, gentle, hungry, unstoppable. We rolled onto the bed and held on to each other like our lives depended on it. I was transported back to the night we had spent together in the kibbutz. I felt that this was the natural continuation of an unfinished story that had begun back then, thousands of miles away.

We shared joy, excitement, calmness, and beauty. I could feel the light touch of his breath on my skin. How does one describe the moment when two people become one? Is it even possible? I felt that every millimeter of my skin was met by every millimeter of his. It was the most absolute sense of being connected; I did not know where my body ended and his began. He let me in as I let him in without reservation or hesitation.

We made love again and again during the night, and finally, as dawn was close, we fell asleep in each other's arms. Late in the morning, we woke up to the sounds of the busy city; we looked at each other and giggled. He leaned towards me, kissed me on the nose and said: "Let's get breakfast. My treat!"

We got out of bed, and he washed himself standing in the large metal bucket. Still naked and dripping wet, he gestured for me to get in with him, and I obliged. He poured water over my head, and I felt like I was standing below a small waterfall. Then he washed me with soapy hands slowly moving all over my body, not missing a spot. I resisted the urge to hold him tight until I stepped out of the bucket onto the soggy carpet. When I finally pressed my body against his, it felt like home.

We finally let go, got dry and dressed, and left the room laughing while running downstairs. On the street, the world of today seemed the same as the world of yesterday, but somehow it felt friendlier. We sat down at the terrace of the corner café, ordered fresh croissants, bread, butter and a pot of coffee. Before André left for school, he asked, "Can I see you tonight?"

I was smiling inside when I nodded. I felt the universe had given us a second chance at love. I watched him walk away and disappear into the crowd.

CHAPTER XIX

A Love Triangle

ANDRÉ and I had now been together for a few months, and our feelings for each other ran much deeper than either of us was willing to verbalize yet. I had fallen in love with him, head over heels this time, and I knew it. In those days "I love you" was not a sentiment often admitted, and we both seemed more comfortable without expressed commitments.

While I wanted to be a part of these unusual times and experience what freedom was all about, I was also very conflicted about it. A lot of young people of our generation lived in communes, sharing everything, from food and housework to clothes, records, and partners. They felt like nothing could ever stop them from leapfrogging over established societal rules. More open and casual relationships were now the new normal.

André liked the idea of me being close with his best friends. We went to parties where we drank vodka, smoked pot, and danced to the enticing rhythms of rock and roll until dawn. It was late into one of these nights that Roger, André's best friend, invited me to his room. Being so close to him felt intoxicating, and I craved his touch on my skin. But, as I was coming down from the highs of the night, the desire that had been there on the dance floor vanished; making love was now just the next step, what was expected. I could not feel anything but pretended as I always did with guys who were "just friends."

Trust played a tremendous role in my ability to be sexual. I trusted André, the way he knew me and understood me. I felt like he knew every inch of my body and I could sense the love in his touch. But passing encounters, even with his best friend, always left me with a sense of sadness that would stick with me for days. When I found myself in a strange bed in the morning, I felt lost, cold, and hurt.

As the months passed, I knew I would soon have another conflict to resolve. When André and I reunited, I had told him about Elias and his expected return, "you and I, it can only be temporary, until he comes back to me," I had announced bravely.

As time went by, the memory of my faraway boyfriend and what we had shared seemed unreal, veiled by the intensity of the present.

At the time, I think André liked the idea of a passing adventure, it was liberating to be together and free at the same time. At the beginning, I honestly thought that my relationship with André was not going to last, but as time went by, and we grew closer to one another, I felt my commitment to Elias fading away.

I had had no direct contact with Elias, but a friend of his had relayed his messages to me. He was turning 21 and would be back in Paris in late April. We were to meet at the hotel room I had booked for him.

Although he was not ready to admit it yet, André's distress about my upcoming encounter was palpable. "Are you sure about this?" he would ask, then he would look away when I had no answer for him.

I knew I needed to see Elias, even if the memories of our time together had lost their colors. I had no idea how I would feel when I met him again. But I had to know if there was anything still alive between us. So, I left André after he made me promise to come back and tell him what had happened. As I closed the door behind me, I caught a glance of him lying in bed, fully clothed, and smoking a cigarette. He was looking straight at me. I had rarely seen the profound sadness I read in his apprehensive brown eyes.

I left him with a heavy heart and walked toward the hotel where Elias was staying. I entered the musty-smelling reception area and climbed the stairs to the second floor. My heart was pounding; I was thrilled and anxious all at once at the thought of him now so close after his long absence. I knocked.

"Come in," he said.

I opened the door and walked into the room. The moment I saw him, everything that had been a blur came into focus again. He was standing by the table, the same tall, slim, dark-haired, brown-eyed, tanned man I remembered.

His expression was hard to read. There was a smile, uncharacteristically shy, in his eyes, but I could detect hurt too. I was sure that he knew about André. I had often noticed his friends when André and I were out and about.

I felt a distance between us, and I did not know how to deal with it, what to do or what to say, so I just stood there, waiting.

"Do you still love me?" he asked.

"Yes," I replied softly, while my eyes were filling with tears.

"Do you love him?" he asked next.

"Yes," I whispered.

He remained quiet for a minute. "What are you going to do now?" he asked, his voice breaking.

"I don't know. But I wanted to see you again ..." My voice trailed off.

I was beginning to understand that life had taken an unexpected turn for all three of us. I realized that someone was going to get hurt, there was no escaping it.

He moved away to the shelf near the sink and began to prepare Turkish coffee with his back to me. From the way his shoulders moved I realized that he was crying quietly.

I crossed the room and encircled his waist with my arms, leaning my cheek against his back. I could hear his heartbeat. He turned around and held my face with his hands and my eyes with his gaze.

"Don't leave me!" he whispered.

I had never heard anyone say this to me, ever. It touched the deepest part of me. How could I ever leave? I think it is at this precise moment that I became trapped in this triangle.

I knew André had something to offer me no other man would ever have. I was still struggling to understand his uncanny abilities to care and to connect with the world and with me. Elias would never be that man. But it is easy to have a 20/20 emotional vision in hindsight. At the time, I was a lost soul in a no man's land, and I didn't even know it.

I heard myself say: "I am here, I am not leaving you." The words tumbled out without a thought. I could not possibly break his heart.

We spent an hour or so drinking coffee, smoking and talking. It was getting late, and André was waiting; I had to go back and tell him something; but I had no idea what. Was it over between us? What was I going to do? I was supposed to say we were over, but I dreaded the thought.

As I slowly walked back to our hotel, I knew I was faced with an impossible choice. With apprehension, I climbed the stairs, knocked, and let myself in. André was still there, still lying on the bed, his head propped up on white pillows, still smoking, an astray full of cigarette butts by his side. He sat up as I settled down on the edge of the bed.

"How did it go?" he asked, like he did not have a worry in the world although the smoke-filled room told a different story.

My throat was tight, and I burst into tears. "I'm leaving", I blurted out unconvincingly.

I was looking down through a rainfall of tears, listening to the silence that followed my words. In my mind, I could picture the tenderness in his eyes.

"You can't do that," he said. The sound of his beautiful voice was unbearable. "I know you love me, and I love you, so why would you go?" he asked.

"You love me? You've never told me this before."

"Taja, you know we're good for each other, we are good together." He could tell that I thought the same. Grabbing my hands: "Stay with me," he said. "I don't want to lose you!"

He pulled me toward him, and we lay down next to each other. He leaned over and kissed me ever so gently on the lips, then he kissed my nose and my forehead. I felt a tear fall on my cheek. I opened my eyes, looked into his and saw everything he had so desperately avoided saying until now.

We made love with emotions running deep. We fell asleep, and I woke up suddenly, remembering that close by Elias was waiting. I got dressed and kissed André. He knew I had to go, but he grabbed my wrist.

"You are coming back, right? Promise?" I nodded and kissed him again before running out.

This back and forth did not bring me closer to a resolution. For two long days, nothing in the world existed for the three of us but the drama playing out in these two hotels rooms. I had never been in a situation where two people wanted and needed me so much; I had never had to make such a heart-breaking choice.

After the second day, André and I ran into a friend of his. When he saw the state, we were in, he asked, "How long has it been since you two had something to eat?"

He took us to lunch at a bistro. Being outside felt so good. It was like we had stepped out of a time machine and were back in the real world. It soothed the pain. It was a sunny day with clouds high in the sky and a breeze that made the tablecloth dance. People were having lunch, the sounds of their lively voices all melted into a comforting soundtrack. The waiter moved around the tables like a ballet dancer. It was all quite entertaining, and somehow, it gave me hope. I turned my head slightly to look at André next to me. His eyes had dark circles underneath, but he was smiling when he looked at me. I think that was when I knew it. It became so clear that my love story with Elias had ended the day he had followed his father back home to Lebanon.

Breaking up with Elias tore me to pieces, but it had to be done. For the next week or so, I felt I was drowning in sadness. André's presence did not help. I felt too disconnected from humankind to be able to let him in, and it took me a while to be able to land back in the real world. But eventually, I did. For André and me, it was a turning point; it was a new beginning of a life committed to each other.

CHAPTER XX

A Weekend in Amsterdam

AMSTERDAM was the European mecca for the free lifestyle of the era. In 1968, the city of Amsterdam had subsidized an abandoned 19th-century building and turned it into a youth center called The Paradiso. It soon became known across Europe that the use of hash and marijuana was allowed there; drugs could be bought and sold and consumed freely without running the risk of being thrown into jail. Students in the Latin Quarter often recounted their trips to Amsterdam, while others fantasized about going. When André left for Switzerland to spend a weekend at Roger's family home, Francis, another friend of ours, invited me on a road trip to Holland. I accepted, loving the idea of a new escapade.

Francis also invited a couple of his close friends, Francois and Anne. The four of us packed a few sweaters and jackets in the back of his car, an old grey *"deux-chevaux"* and took off, driving north towards Belgium on small icy roads. The atmosphere on the road was joyous; our hearts were filled with excitement. We kept driving until we reached our destination, stopping only for coffee to stay awake.

We arrived in Amsterdam late at night and found a room in a youth hostel; it had two sets of bunk beds with army blankets covering the mattresses. Tired after the long drive, we each grabbed a bed and lay down, eyes shut for the night. I was woken up a few times by visitors' coughing, laughing, and their heavy steps in and out of the rooms next to us. The walls between rooms were paper thin but I finally slept.

I was alone in the room when I woke up the next day. *"They must have gone for breakfast,"* I thought. I waited for a while, and then decided to wash up in the tiny sink. Refreshed, I put on my favorite light blue jeans, the dark blue sweater borrowed from André and slipped my feet into thick knitted socks and my Swedish clogs. On my way out, I picked up my white sheepskin coat, the wool on the inside keeping me warm. I ran downstairs, bumping into a few long-haired, bearded hippies who mumbled something I did not understand. I thought it must have been a greeting.

I started walking down the street, looking around at the rundown buildings under the gray sky. Amsterdam was a strange city. I had only seen it once before, when traveling with Damien and Reine. Nothing here now reminded me of the beautiful images I had kept from before of colorful flowers lining the balconies, of orderly buildings overlooking neat, clean streets, and the canals, their still waters reflecting the pale blue sky.

Suddenly, I noticed my friends coming toward me.

"Hey, do you know what time it is?" Francis asked, grinning. I had no idea. "It's past two o'clock!"

"Are you hungry?" I nodded.

"Let's get a bite to eat and then head toward the Paradiso. I think it opens at five."

After a couple of hours at a café, we headed towards the youth center. As we walked, night was falling, and the air gradually became colder. We arrived in front of a massive structure that looked like an old church and a factory merged into one. Anne and I stood at the huge arched front door while the guys were purchasing hashish from dealers; it was all in the open, everyone around was totally relaxed about it.

As we entered the building, I could see a wide door opening onto a room with ceilings so high it could have been a train station. The lights were sparse and dim. Creedence Clearwater Revival's "Run through the Jungle" was playing so loud it seemed to fill the entire space from floor to ceiling. The rhythm was irresistible. I felt transported, amazed by the beat I felt from head to toe. The dance floor was empty except for a tall and slim man with long dark hair. He was wearing jeans, a dark shirt, high boots, and a long duster. His whole body was moving to the music. Nothing in the world seemed to exist but the pure ecstasy and freedom with which he moved. I was hypnotized; I had never seen anyone that free before. At that moment, all I wanted was to be him.

But my lifestyle of reckless abandon and living as if there were no tomorrows abruptly ended the day I came back from that weekend in Amsterdam. The night before, Francis and I had purchased what we thought was pure marijuana. But it must have been laced with an unknown ingredient. Whatever it was remained a mystery, but it caused a seemingly never-ending night of terror, which I think permanently damaged the gates behind which my trauma lived. I will never forget tripping all night in terrifying uncharted territories of violently distorted perceptions. Curled up together, we barely talked but hung on to each other like we were the only two living beings left on earth. All we could do was wait, looking at his watch every so often convinced hours had gone by when, in fact, only minutes had passed.

As we were on our way home, Anne lost control of the car on the icy roads, and we careened onto two wheels. As my three companions were screaming, I watched the scene unfolding in slow motion. My hypervigilance pushed me into action, and, in a flash, I reached over from the backseat, grabbed the wheel, and steered us back to safety.

Exhausted from the night ride on the icy roads of Belgium and northern France, I walked in, dropped my bag, and just lay down. But I could not sleep. I turned to my side. My eyes were studying the motifs on the faded carpet, when suddenly, I thought I saw myself there on the floor, lying in a pool of blood. The scene was fascinating, vivid, three-dimensional, and too real. So where was I? Which version of me was the real one? Was it me on the bed, or was I on the floor?

I could not tell.

PANIC

My first panic attack happened on the night after I returned from Amsterdam. André and I were on our way to have dinner at a local bistro. As we walked out, I said something to tease him. He smiled, then made a funny face and jokingly put his hands around my neck as if he intended to strangle me. Playfully, I started running down the stairs, but I accidentally missed a step - or thought I did.

Terror struck.

That night I felt the ground open under my feet, but I managed to grab the banister. My heart was pounding in my chest, but instead of slowing down when I retrieved my balance it raced faster, ever faster. The danger had passed, but my brain and my body did not seem to register that fact. In seconds, waves of fear invaded every square inch of my body, sending me to the floor shaking uncontrollably, teeth chattering, certain that I was dying.

There are eyes scanning every inch inside my body, looking for the slightest signal of a strange sensation, a twitch, a click indicating I have finally stepped on a mine. I am waiting for what is to come, what cannot be avoided. Is this how it was meant to end all along? I am shaking like a leaf, then I stop, stiffen my muscles, and hold my breath. My eyes are as wide as saucers. My arms are wrapped tight against my stomach to try and stop that awful tension in my diaphragm that I believe will soon prevent the natural flow of my breath.

What if I cannot breathe? What if my muscles stop moving? What if my brain shuts down? What if ...? The more I try to get away from one of these scary thoughts, the faster another catches up with me, always more terrifying and more merciless than the preceding one.

195

Fear infiltrates every cell, and all I can do is answer the ancient call of my brainstem: get up and run. But there is nothing to run away from. I feel like a cartoon character who jumped over a cliff but does not fall until it looks down. I must not look down. I must not look down! I must keep on running ...

I wonder if this terror has a name. Because if it does, maybe I could speak to it, pray for mercy, pray for the end of pain, for my life back. I could beg it to stop hurting me, to leave me alone, to keep me safe, please, please. I'll do anything, I promise.

The terror only got worse as thoughts of inner devastation ran through my head. I was disconnected, floating into space, about to be lost forever. There was a monster inside me, implacable, unforgiving. It was taking me away from my life, my love, my world.

I did not realize then that my life had changed forever. I had no idea that the haunting panic that possessed me that night was going to stalk and shadow me at every turn. I understood only much later that the terror had been present, living underground inside me, only held back by a dam with faulty construction. It had been dormant like a volcano until its inevitable eruption on that fatal evening in Amsterdam. And when it finally blew up, it killed everything in its path, my hopes, my freedom, and the promise of a meaningful future I intended to build.

Panic attacks kept coming at me with a vengeance. From that evening on, my primary goal in life was to find a way to control the monster inside, to satisfy its hunger in the hope of taming it. No one, friends or professionals, understood what was happening to me; it was too intangible. Medical testing and evaluations were performed and shed no light on the issue. Over the following years, family, and even medical professionals reacted with irritation or anger each time they witnessed my panic attacks. They saw it as a setup, a manipulation on my part to get attention. If only they had known. I still feel their suspicious and judgmental eyes on me while, curled up in the corner of a room, I am unable to do anything but talk to the terror and ask it to stop. I just needed one kind word, but there was none.

Much later, I heard an interview with a gentleman about his own experiences with panic attacks. During World War II, he had been one of the many soldiers who landed on the beaches of Normandy on D-Day. He said, "I cannot find a better way to explain what a panic attack feels like other than to say that if you offered me a choice between going back to that beach on D-Day or a panic attack, I'd always choose D-Day."

His words stayed with me. He was a brave American soldier who had fought to defeat Hitler and rescue Europe from the Nazis. Nothing about him was weak. A long-time sufferer of PTSD, he just spoke the truth. Hearing him talk, I felt less alone, less shamed by unkind and unsympathetic witnesses who saw my panic as a manipulative behavior rather than what it was, an uncontrollable and life-altering out-of-the-blue terror.

~ REFLECTIONS & INSIGHTS ~

Looking back later, I realized that when I left home, I was lost in the world with nowhere to go, without resources. Terror had been part of my life as a child abandoned and brutalized in foster homes, then at home around Damien. After I liberated myself from him and life at home, although I did not know it at the time, the world out there terrified me. This led me to drinking and smoking pot to lose myself, to reach a fear-free state, and mostly forget the sadness and the shame. And it worked, for a while. But somehow these substances chipped away at the fragile defenses that kept my horrific memories buried.

The old stories began to play like a film, frame by frame, inside my head. But that terror and the myriads of feelings I had experienced as a young child were still separated, unavailable, concealed in my unconscious. So, when the first panic attack descended upon my life, I had no understanding of its meaning, or of the concept and mechanism of faulty gating that Art Janov would later write about.

I was not then able to make a connection between the pure horror of this first attack and the event that preceded my birth. It was years later that I realized that just like my mother had skipped a step and fallen down the stairs on the day I was born, I had missed a step - or thought I did. The true context for the terror in these attacks was that original fall teetering on the edge of my consciousness.

The two falls were carbon copies of one another, so as consciousness returned, there emerged a bridge between the two events, reuniting them, giving them a continuity that had escaped me until many years later in therapy, circumstances triggered the full-blown recollection of that original experience.

But André believed me, stood by me and he saved me. He never gave up hope that there was a way out of my nightmare. So, I kept going. Today, I feel that without this one human being who did not shy away from stepping into my world, I might have taken my life to stop the terror but even more so, to escape the isolation in which the world had left me.

Over the years, I became split inside, having so many personas to take care of day in, day out. One was the fighter, at war with her inner demons; another was the survivor, busy leading a normal life, hiding the disease she had become ashamed of, feeling like a leper on the inside. Yet another kept wishing to die, victimized by intolerance and ignorance, struggling with all her might to overcome the never-ending rejection and humiliation.

CHAPTER XXI

Free Love Comes at a Price

SOME TIME LATER, I found a cheap room in the ancient servant quarters of an old building close to Rue de Reaumur, on a small street in an area where prostitutes hung out; their cheerful banter uplifted my spirits. The room was a shoebox, but it was *my* shoebox. There was just enough space for a single bed and a sink with a window just above it, opening onto a small piece of sky. André came to spend the night often.

At the time, I was working in the Latin Quarter at a *crepe* booth right across from the Sorbonne. I was dreaming of studying medicine to become a psychiatrist, but I could not afford to go to school. Then I heard that poor students could apply for some help from the government. It was a pittance, but it helped to pay for books and expenses, and sometimes, it would be enough for a student to survive on a part-time job. Encouraged by André, I went to the financial aid department to apply for a grant.

The financial aid office requested that I present proof of my parents' income. Getting help depended on whether they had the means to support me. Discouraged, I gave up on the idea of going to school for the time being. I did not want to have anything to do with Damien or Reine. I knew that one way or another, Damien would sabotage my chances of entering university.

So, I went on working at dead-end jobs that I would often quit when I had a little money. It was Saturday, and I had not worked for a week. André was not around, and I felt miserable and isolated, so I got dressed and ran downstairs. As usual, I was greeted by my two favorite prostitutes, who were always hanging out by the front door of my building.

I was in the mood to walk so I followed Rue de Reaumur all the way and turned right toward the Latin Quarter. Minutes later, I found myself out on Boulevard Saint-Michel. It was the weekend, and the cafes were crowded, and so was the boulevard. The crowds were a mix of students and families out for the night, on their way to a movie or a play.

The light from cafés and closed stores illuminated the curb, and it reflected on the chrome of the passing cars and buses. I started up the boulevard on the right side, careful not to bump into the crowd. People coming from behind would occasionally bump into me while rushing up to wherever they were going. I moved closer to the buildings to get away and kept walking. After leaving most of the cafes behind, the crowds thinned. I made it to the small street that cut into the boulevard. At its corner was one of my favorite Chinese restaurants, where André and I often ate when we went out.

I looked up and froze. Right in front of me, lit by a streetlamp was André with a blonde girl. They were kissing. She was wrapped in his arms, and they looked like they had forgotten the world around them.

I instinctively moved into the shadow of a building. Mesmerized, I just stood there. Merciless waves of despair were passing through me one after the other. Before they could spot me, I turned my back to them and ran back home as if someone was out to get me, wound me, torture me. I ran into the building, up the stairs, rushed inside my door and slammed it shut, leaning against it for a moment while catching my breath.

I was as surprised as I was hurt. I had no idea that André was seeing someone else. My world was collapsing fast, but there was nothing to do other than lie down, light a joint, and stare at the ceiling until I felt anesthetized enough to not feel that horrible pain that made me want to die. But it did not work. I could only think about the things I loved about André, every little detail of his appearance, the way he was with me. My desire, my hunger, my need for him was consuming me. The thought of losing his love was unbearable. I could not imagine my life without him.

I began to cry, my chest torn apart, my heart heavy. I cried until I had no more tears, but the pain was still there. So, I just lay there waiting for nothing, hoping for nothing.

I must have dozed off because I was woken up by a knock on the door, two feet away from my pillow. My eyes were swollen, and I did not want to open them. I wanted to stay right where I was forever. I did not move and did not make a sound, but the knocking persisted. Then I heard André's voice.

"Taja, it's me, open the door." I was completely silent. "Please, open up," he insisted. "I know you are in there."

I wondered how he could possibly know that I was here. I thought he might have spoken to one of the prostitutes who had seen me run back in.

I had to say something. "Go away, just go away!"

"What's happening? Why are you crying? Taja, let me in," he pleaded. He had no intention of going away. He sat down on the floor on the other side of the door. I did not know what to do.

"Just go away! I saw you!" I cried out.

"You saw me?" He sounded puzzled.

"Yes, I saw you kissing that blond girl." I started sobbing again. "Please, just leave me alone."

He was quiet for a moment, but he was still there. I was now sitting on the floor, my head against the door, and I could hear him breathe on the other side.

"I am not leaving until you let me in," he said. I could not keep the tears from rolling down to the floor. He must have heard me. "Let me in," he said, but this time he sounded broken too.

I got up and opened the door. He had stood up too and his hands were resting on the door jamb above his head. There was so much sadness in his eyes it broke my heart. I feared what he was about to tell me. My whole body tensed, and I closed my eyes preparing for the blow of his words. The pain that had been inside for an eternity was now finally catching up with me. I was going to be swept away by it, killed by it, but I did not care.

Suddenly, I felt his arms around me, and with one of his hands he lifted my chin so my eyes would meet his. "Look at me," he said. "I love you."

I knew his eyes could not lie. I held on to him. I could not speak, I could not move, we just stood there in the doorway. Slowly, he led me into the room and closed the door. We sat on my bed.

"I had no idea it would hurt you so much," he began. "You've been out with other guys, and I am okay with that. I thought you felt the same."

"I don't know. I just saw you with her and you looked so ... so much in love," I said looking down because when I looked at him, I felt a dam was about to break inside.

"No, no," he said, grabbing my chin again gently. "She is a friend of Roger's. I met her in Switzerland, and she is in Paris for a few days. We fooled around, and I like her, but she does not mean the same to me as you do. It is not like you and me, and it will never be."

His words were reassuring, and I knew he meant what he said. I trusted him.

But I was still shaken up. I heard myself say, "It's okay for you to see another ... friend ..." I could not bring myself to say the word *girlfriend*.

"What's her name?" I asked.

"Judith," he replied.

I hesitated, then continued. "I just don't want to lose you, that's all," I said quietly.

These were the days of sexual liberation and experimentation with relationships. In truth, it frightened me. But, when I was intoxicated, what was it that pushed me into the arms of others? Did I get high to be able to behave as was expected of me, to feel I belonged to my generation? Or was it because I felt there was never enough love, enough attention, enough touch?

Whatever it was, I always felt I was on the edge of a cliff, looking for a way to end the hurt and find inner peace. And for reasons I could not understand then, I felt the only way to find that inner tranquility was to jump into the abyss, no matter how dangerous it was.

I knew that sharing André would hurt, but I felt I had no choice.

*

It must have been during spring break, around five o'clock in the morning, after one of our long nights out, when I came up with the idea of hitchhiking down south to the Riviera.

"Now?" André asked.

"Why not?" I asked. "Why end the fun?"

The idea was catching on, and if my friends had had any objections at first, these were quickly discarded. We all went back to our respective homes to grab a few essentials, toothbrushes, and bathing suits, then headed to the edge of Paris on the first subway train. From then on, we would hitchhike. In those days, hitchhiking was a common way for students to travel, a luxury that they could not otherwise afford.

We picked a spot where the first who made it down to the coast would wait for the others. We knew that there was a small park just behind a hotel where we had stayed in the past. We could not afford a hotel this time around. So, a couple of the guys carried small tents that we were hoping to set up as close to the beach as possible.

By now, Judith and I had become closer. We decided to travel together, and it did not take long before we were picked up by a trucker. We never waited too long between rides. Still, it was well past ten o'clock at night when we made it to our destination. The small park was just the way I remembered it, and at this time of night, it was only lit by a few streetlamps. We both crashed on a bench, exhausted but happy and hungry. After the many hours spent in trucks with deafening engines, the quiet in the park was welcome.

Half an hour later, we decided to go to a local café. We needed to stay awake until at least one of the others arrived. We ordered coffee and just sat there quietly, looking into the night, listening to the gentle ebb and flow of the sea.

"I can't wait until sunrise," I said, and Judith nodded.

We sipped our drinks, paid our waiter, and decided to head back to the park. No one had made it to the rendezvous spot just yet. There was nothing to do but wait. As time passed, we began to ask ourselves what could have possibly held them back. It was almost one o'clock. Judith and I tried to keep our growing anxiety at bay by imagining silly scenarios that would explain the delayed meeting. We were wide awake now. Around two o'clock, I finally said out loud what we had both been thinking about for a while.

"What if they had an accident?" I felt a sense of dread as I spoke. Out loud, the possibility had become more than that, much closer to a reality. I had never been afraid to lose André to a premature death before. It was unthinkable.

"No way," Judith said. "Trucks are a pretty safe way to travel," she added as if she was trying to convince herself.

Waiting felt like torture. As the clock rang three o'clock in the morning, my fear climbed to impossible heights. I was now sure something terrible had happened. Fear turned into despair that entered every cell of my body. Judith looked worried sick.

I was watching the dark intently, but I could not see anything. My eyes were full of tears, blurring everything I looked at. My hope was drifting away as minutes passed. Then suddenly, I heard footsteps coming towards us. I looked up and saw him through my tears. André! He was walking towards us accompanied by a guy he had befriended while hitching a ride. I jumped up and ran up to him, he grabbed me and held me tight.

In the morning, we set up camp under the pine trees. André and I shared a small tent, but I hardly spent time in it; I just loved falling asleep under the stars even when the temperature dropped by the end of the night. I wrapped myself in blankets and waited for the sun to climb and set the Eastern horizon on fire.

One morning, I went for a long walk along the shore. When I got back, I walked up to our little blue tent intending to curl up next to André for a while only to find him with Judith wrapped in his arms kissing him passionately.

And that's when it happened. That hurt too deep to bear. And, just like that, I knew I was done with free love. I picked up my meager belongings, shoved them into my backpack and walked away without uttering a word. Just like when I had left home, I knew that I was done with that lifestyle, regardless of the consequences. The thought that I could walk away from André had never crossed my mind before, but now I felt that pain was going to end me. And I was shocked to realize how much I wanted to be free of that hurt that infiltrated every part of my being.

As I reached the road, I heard footsteps approaching, felt his hands on my shoulders, and his arms wrap themselves around me. I could not turn around. Holding back the tears, I whispered: "I cannot do this anymore!"

My throat felt so tight it was hard to breathe. But he would not let go, so I turned to face him and look in his beautiful sad eyes and said: "You and I, we're over." It broke my heart to see the pain in them.

I looked away. I did not know if I even believed my own words. I would have sold my soul not to lose him. But there was a resolve inside I could neither deny nor hold back.

The light in his eyes turned a few shades darker. He must have understood what was happening because his grip on me tightened.

"We are together. It's just you and me now."

He took my hand, and we headed back to camp. Judith was sitting on the sand, sipping coffee from a broken mug. She looked up at us both and got up. She gave me a hug and smiled, gestured goodbye, and walked away to the sea, her long blond hair floating gracefully as she moved.

Back in Paris, André and I moved in together. My cousin Sabine and her husband had just moved into a new apartment in the eleventh arrondissement, close to Place de la République, on the second story of a small old stone building, and they were looking for someone to share the rent with.

The windows in our room opened onto a quiet and picturesque courtyard. There was a bed in a corner and shelves on the opposite side. We brushed a coat of fresh white paint on the oak wainscot and stapled undyed jute fabric to cover the upper part of the walls. André brought in an impressive number of books. Above the small table I hung a couple of posters: Freud and a Magritte reproduction of a house at dusk. This was home now. André went back to university, and I found my first real full-time job with a company I had never heard of, Dun and Bradstreet.

CHAPTER XXII

Someone Found,

Someone Lost

AT THE END of spring in 1972, as Parisians were emerging, in recovery mode after the long dark nights of winter, gray skies, and unending rainy days, there was a lightness in the air; the sun's rays lasted longer and grew warmer as they hit the rooftops and the café terraces even during the downpour of intermittent showers. It was not time for the longed-for summer days and southern retreats just yet. Regardless, anticipation put a bounce in their steps.

I had not seen Reine and Damien in a long time, but unexpectedly, they reached out. They had hired a private detective who eventually did find me. They hoped I would agree to a meeting, but my

211

first reaction was to ignore their request. What good could it do me? But my life had changed. I was not alone. I had the support of André and our friends, we had a place to live, I had a steady job where my work was appreciated.

But I still feared them; I wondered if I was strong enough to face the assault of their baseless judgments and criticisms, and what these would awaken in me. What if it sent me into another bout of despair? But in the end curiosity prevailed.

André and Roger were well aware of my parents' shortcomings, especially when contrasted with their own parents. I loved them for standing by my side the day I met Reine and Damien. I introduced everyone. André and Roger looked perfect, well behaved, educated, and polite, but there was something in their eyes and demeanor that gave my parents pause; a warning for them to be on their best behavior.

We went to a local café for a late breakfast. I do not remember saying much, content to just observe the interactions. I was biting into a fresh croissant when I was struck by the expression on my mother's face. There was so much sadness in her eyes. Was it the result of my rejection and prolonged absence? Had she been the one to initiate the search to find me? The tension between Damien and Reine was unmistakable. When we said our goodbyes, my mother was reluctant to leave; she held my hands a bit longer, as if she wished to delay the separation. But when André put his arm around me, she let go, and we walked away.

Some time had elapsed before my mother called André to invite us and his parents for a Sunday at their house in Dammarie. André and I were due to leave the city and be on our way to Spain for a long summer away, just the two of us. The invitation appealed to everyone as did the forest's fresh air. Dammarie seemed like a good place for this highly unusual meeting, the first of its kind.

The mood was cordial. The families got along well and enjoyed a late lunch in the beautiful garden under the silver birch trees. There were splashes of vivid reds, pinks, corals, and yellows scattered everywhere, as the tulips my mother had planted were now in full bloom. The day went by peacefully, interrupted now and then by a peal of laughter. I truly hoped for this day to be the dawning of a *détente* in our relationship in our relationship. Was it possible that my parents' feelings toward me had changed?

Before we left, Damien and Reine invited me to spend a week's vacation in the South where they had reserved a suite in a hotel set in a pretty town in the mountains somewhere in the Pyrenees for early August. Since it was so close to the Spanish border, we decided that André would join me a few days later, and from there we would take a train to the South of Spain.

*

The small town was quaint and peaceful, redolent of centuries past, set in the midst of deep green hills that evoked velvet blankets spreading far against a stunning backdrop of jagged rocks. As I walked to the public pool each day, I detoured via mountain trails to immerse myself in the scenery, the intensity of colors, the deep blue up above, the many shades of greens and the freshness in the air of these early summer mornings. High up in the distance, the soft musical sounds of bells ringing could be heard, faint and dreamy as goats and cows moved around in the fields.

I spent most of my time at the pool or walking around town with joyful anticipation as I waited for André. At the hotel, Damien and Reine were fighting, my mother verbally violent and loud at times, so much so that hotel guests had complained about the noise.

A few days later, we all went for a hike in the rugged mountains. We did not walk for long before the sky turned from blue to gray in a matter of minutes. As we were climbing down the rocky dirt path, suddenly in the far distance, we heard the inescapable deep long distress call of an alpine horn that filled the valley below announcing lost or hurt hikers. I was immediately enveloped in a feeling of dread. It stayed with me as we made it back to the hotel. The skies had turned dark, and rain was pouring down.

I began to fear that there was a hidden meaning behind the sound of the alpine horn and the weather turning dark and threatening, as if they were harbingers of doom. The conviction that André's life was about to end overpowered me. Was this a premonition? I did not know, but I could not stop the tears running down my cheeks.

I tried to telephone home a few times, hoping André or Stéphane, his younger brother, would answer; the phone would ring on and on, but no one picked up. Their parents had flown to Morocco for their holidays, so I couldn't reach them either.

As André did not arrive a day or so later, I caught a train ride back to Paris. As the train sped through the night, I began to feel calm, almost uplifted. The dread had fully dissipated when the train snaked into Gare de Lyon.

Once back home I ran up the steps and let myself in. I found Stéphane asleep and woke him up. As he slowly came to, he looked at me in surprise.

"What are you doing here!?"

"André did not show up! Do you know when he left?"

"I'm not sure ..." Stéphane looked perplexed, not quite fully awake.

"Why don't you get up? I'll make coffee," I said.

A moment later, he was sipping hot black coffee out of André's mug.

"Let's go to your parents' apartment in case there are news from André there," I suggested.

We were a few subway stations away, so the ride was quick, and we were back above ground only minutes later. We walked around the Place de la Nation to the imposing stone building, rang the bell, and the concierge appeared, a puzzled smile on her face as she recognized us.

I blurted out: "I can't find André! I wondered ... Have you received any news?"

She noticed my anxious expression and exclaimed: "No, no, don't you worry! I'm sure there is no cause for alarm. I would have been informed!"

We thanked her and left, heading back toward the subway station, but we still had no idea where André was. I thought he might have finally arrived at my parents' hotel to find that I was back in Paris, looking for him. As we descended toward the hot air blowing from the subway, a thought crossed my mind.

"Weren't your parents going to move to that new apartment soon?"

"They have already moved most of their stuff there," Stéphane replied. "It's a work in progress, there are still some things they'll have to take care of when they get back from vacation."

A distressing thought jumped into my mind. "Let's go there and check, maybe the concierge will know something." "They could have made the change of address with the postal service, couldn't they?"

Stéphane looked doubtful but followed my lead. We walked a few blocks, turned to the right, and arrived in front of a modern and classy apartment building. The front door was made of glass. Seconds after we rang the bell, a concierge appeared and opened the door.

Stéphane introduced himself. I thought I read apprehension in the concierge's eyes, but I did not know the woman. She walked to the elevator and pressed the button. Then she just said: "The doctor has been expecting you."

We stepped in and pressed the button. As we landed, a heavy mahogany door opened, and a woman with a welcoming smile who must have been the doctor's wife rushed us into the dining room and said: "The doctor will be right with you!"

Seconds later, an older man in a suit, with gray hair and heavy glasses walked in. I could not read him. Then he spoke without emotion: "I am sorry to inform you that André has been wounded in an accident."

"Where is he? Which hospital?" I asked. "I must see him, I have to go, now!!"

Then the word I had skipped over now reached my consciousness "… André has been *fatally* wounded in an accident."

That word hit me. It was brutal, merciless, inhuman, impossible. *No, no, no, no* … I felt myself falling, engulfed by ruthless terror, my hands grabbed the table in front of me to steady myself.

The pain of loss was unbearable. I felt myself separating from reality. Images of my vibrant boyfriend flashed by, on and on and on, each tearing me to shreds. We would never hold each other again, never smile together, never hold hands, never sleep in each other's arms, I would never again breathe in the scent of his silky hair, never, ever, ever, ever. OMG! No, no, no, no …. Someone wake me up, please, please … Suddenly, I felt enveloped by a white veil that hid the world around me. It touched me lightly, protected me by fading the intensity of colors, scents, and sounds, but not entirely. The tear of loss was still in me, but its sharp edges mercifully softened. I wondered where Stéphane was, and then I saw him beside me, inside the veil as he reached for my hand.

CHAPTER XXIII

Trapped in Trauma

IT WAS THE SUMMER of 1972. I was standing beneath the tall plane trees, cut off from the rest of humanity. In this moment of unbearable pain, a new sensation was emerging in me – something intense, a joy born from the certainty that nature around me was alive, vibrant. It instilled my body with its molecules, diluting the sadness and restoring a sense of belonging that had been gone since the moment André's death had been announced.

But now I could feel life throbbing in my temples. The rustle of a million leaves became a familiar language, they all whispered softly in the summer breeze. The branches were moving endlessly, and even the shadows seemed hospitable. The colors were deep and delicate: no artist's hand would ever be able to reproduce the perfection I was absorbing. The asphalt burnt through my soles, and the heat enveloped my pain, taking me to a state of anesthesia where the only important thing was to not let this connection with André escape. I still felt his presence all around me.

A shiny black car slowed down and stopped next to us, and we got in. The car slowly rode along the sleepy streets of Père Lachaise Cemetery. At the chapel, two sad-looking men carried a long wooden box from the car and lowered it down on the gravel. I closed my eyes as an almost irresistible desire grabbed hold of me to kneel next to the box and enclose it tenderly in my arms, a final protective gesture.

Led by one of the men, our small group left the sunlight to enter the darkness of the chapel. Gradually, a few rows of lined-up chairs became visible as my eyes adjusted to the dark. There were sounds of shuffling boots on the old stone tiles, of chairs scratching the floor, a few discreet coughs, a few words whispered, and then silence. The first measures of Beethoven's *Ninth Symphony* exploded. Stéphane, André's brother, took my hand and squeezed it hard. I turned to him: I would have thought he was made of wax if I had not glimpsed the despair in his eyes that looked so much like those of his brother.

I turned my attention towards the wall before me. I pictured the flames licking the edges, climbing, spreading, slowly devouring the whole wall. Amid the blaze, I could see André, eyes closed, face relaxed, his beautiful silky black hair floating around it. I wanted to touch him. I wanted to feel the navy-blue jacket that he had just bought that looked so good on him. I wanted to smell his leather belt with its worn patina one last time. But all of it was burning, and I was so afraid that he would feel the pain of his burning flesh. The thought was horrendous. All I could hang on to was the power of the music and Stéphane's hand holding mine.

Suddenly the music that had filled the space ended.

We walked to a door hidden behind a pillar towards André's final resting place. As we began to step down a broad staircase that led underground, two men joined us, carrying a tiny stretcher, with a small box made of stone on it. I stared, understanding escaping me. Then the word "ashes" reached my consciousness and what it meant imposed itself. How could I ever convey in words the immensity of loss, of a connection with another being that ran so deep it became part of my core?

It was final. Something inside me was torn irreparably and forever.

The small black procession began to descend. At the foot of the stone staircase, we turned left, right, and left again. The walls were covered with slabs of black and white marble, inscriptions, and a vase of flowers of all colors, some freshly cut, some wilted. Finally, we stopped in front of a small open space. The small stone box was slipped into the hole, the hole was covered with a marble plate, black, polished, with words engraved on it in golden letters. The plate was sealed, and the ceremony ended.

We climbed back up and stepped into the graveyard bathed in gentle light. Birds were chirping, a few old people were taking their afternoon walk. Tourists gathered around the graves of famous artists cast curious eyes over us.

*

In the weeks following André's burial, I stayed with his parents. Both Becca and Stéphane Sr. welcomed me into their home. It was more than a welcome; it was first and foremost a way to keep the connection to their son alive.

Becca said once: "If you were pregnant, I'd grab this child and would raise him for you!"

I heard the question and the hope in her voice. The word "him" struck me as odd, but then I understood that I was the link between her and her son. A way not to let go, not really. Had I been pregnant, André's son would have filled the empty space left in her heart.

My presence was also a way to stay focused on the mundane, keeping them busy, and maintaining a routine to prevent a complete collapse. Nevertheless, the grief would sometimes send them both into hiding in the bathroom or the bedroom where I could hear their heart-wrenching sobs that would die down after a while. Then they would come out, struggling to put on a brave face again.

NIGHTMARE: ANDRÉ'S RETURN

After André's death, a recurring nightmare began to torment me. Some details changed from time to time, but the events of the dream always followed the same terrible path. There was a party going on at my parents' old apartment in Noisy, and André had come back. He was not dead! Of all places, my parents' apartment was a strange choice for a venue, but I thought little of it; I could not wait to see him again. I did not question his reappearance amongst the living. All that mattered was that he was alive and well, and that soon I would be in his arms, touching his face, smelling his hair, seeing his smile again. Life was going to change; it was going to be a dream all over again.

I was standing by the door, my finger on the bell. I could hear the muffled chatter behind it. Unable to delay another second, I rang and immediately heard steps coming towards me. I did not recognize the man in front of me, but he invited me in with a smile.

I saw people everywhere; some of them were clear and defined, but a few looked like shadowy ghosts, although they were part of the crowd and interacted with others just as much as anyone else. There was excitement in the air; the news of André's return had brought many, many friends here, together with family. Strangely enough, I did not recognize anyone.

My eyes were scanning the room, trying to locate André. I recognized his profile right away. He was deep in conversation surrounded by a group of people who seemed attentive to his every word. He had not seen me yet. I approached him without rushing, but my heart was beating fast. I was right behind him, close enough to touch him but I did not. Instead, I spoke softly.

"André, it's me," I whispered.

He did not react. I thought the noise had covered my voice, so I tried again. "André, it's me, Taja," I said softly but louder.

He did not turn around, so this time I tapped his shoulder and said, "Turn around! Please!"

That did not work either. He would not stop the conversation he was engaged in, and he would not turn around to face me. Suddenly, I knew with the most absolute certainty: he did not want to see me. He knew I was standing right behind him but chose to ignore me.

223

Something must have happened, and he did not love me anymore; he wanted me to realize that and just go away.

There were no words that could have expressed the depth of my despair. It was the most intolerable pain I had ever felt, and I knew I could not bear it, I knew there was no way to continue living with it. I begged André to turn around and look at me one last time. When he did not turn to me, there was only one thing to do; I had to stop the pain raging inside me at all costs.

Like a trapped animal, I looked to the right toward what used to be my room and caught a glimpse of the large bay window. Without a thought, I ran as fast as I could and jumped through the glass. In slow motion I saw the glass break into a million pieces and float in the air in every direction all around me. I saw the ground far down below. I started to go down, and I screamed, "I made a mistake! I don't want to die!" But it was too late.

I thought I emerged from the nightmare and cried out.

But then, in bed beside me, André jumped, shocked out of a deep sleep. He did not say a word but quickly switched on the side lamp that shed a soft light around the room. He took me in his arms gently and whispered reassuring words. The many, many years of nocturnal terror had left me frozen like a wax doll, time after time. I opened my eyes and let myself feel his presence, absorb the peacefulness that came from him, and burrowed my face in his arms. He watched me fall asleep again, calmer now, although my fists were still so tightly clenched that he did not manage to grab hold of my hand.

And then, I woke up.

I was losing him over and over again; there was no escape from the desolate landscape inside me.

SLEEP THERAPY

In the time that followed Andre's death, panic attacks sent me to the hospital emergency room so often I might as well have been living there. No one understood what I was going through although the doctors and nurses were always patient and kind. They witnessed my distress, proof that something was wrong; my blood pressure climbed awfully high, my heart rate galloped like a racehorse. I would rock back and forth and curl up to catch my breath. The sensations were terrifying. I was a mess.

The doctors injected doses of Valium I suspect could have felled a horse, but my body fought against the calming substance. The shaking would not stop. My teeth chattered so hard I thought they would break. It felt like forever until the terror had run its course and finally dissipated. Another narrow escape from Hell ... All I could do was to just lie there, exhausted but alive. A sense of peace would descend upon me and bring me to tears. And then I would hear the melody of a song by Jean Ferrat. Its words echoed my thoughts. *"All that trembles and throbs / All that struggles and fights / All that I thought too soon was forever lost / All that is given back / How beautiful life is, how beautiful ..."*

*

I had an appointment with a psychiatrist at a clinic in the suburbs. His name was Dr. Renoir. I arrived on time and was invited to wait next to the imposing doorway. It was an old building that had seen better days. The hall was very tall, the walls painted off-white, the floor, presumably original, was covered in once colorful geometric art deco tiles, now faded and cracked here and there.

A voice called my name. I looked up and saw a tall, slim blond man in a crumpled beige suit, too big for him, floating around his frame as he walked. His face reminded me of Serge Gainsbourg's, not because he looked like him, but because he looked like he could have used a good night's sleep. The way he moved indicated that he was in his early 40s, but his face looked at least 20 years older. His eyes were kind, and I took an instant liking to him.

We entered his office. He sat behind a desk, grabbed a pack of cigarettes that lay next to him and lit one while grasping at an ashtray already half full of cigarette butts. I liked him even more.

He asked me the usual questions, showed a keen interest, and offered to keep me at the clinic for a while to run some tests and then to stay for what was called a *"cure de sommeil."* During this treatment, sleep was induced with pills or shots for as long as necessary. He recommended a two-to-three-week-long sleep treatment to help me recover. He thought that sleep would help me regain my strength and offer my nervous system a chance to "regroup." I welcomed the idea.

I came back later that week. I was shown to the room where I would spend the rest of my stay. It was cold, the furniture sparse, but the large window overlooked a magnificent park with long stretches of green grass and massive, old chestnut and oak trees that made me feel like running out and climbing up to the protective shelter of their branches and leaves that were beginning to turn a rusty color.

I was left to put my few belongings in a closet and change into pajamas that smelled clean and fresh. Soon, a nurse came in and closed the shutters. The room was almost completely dark now except for slivers of daylight where the slats of the shutters did not meet. Dr. Renoir came in, asked me if I was ready, and I nodded. Sitting on the edge of the narrow bed, he wrapped my arm tight in a rubber band, tapped my skin a few times, and proceeded to give me a shot I hardly felt at all.

I welcomed the darkness and the wonderful feeling of peace that was embracing me, spreading fast from cell to cell in my body. I was smiling on the inside. At long last, I was safe. Gradually, I drifted into a deep, long, comatose sleep.

Without warning, daylight flooded the room. When I saw the nurse opening the shutters, I thought to myself, *there must have been a mistake, I just fell asleep. Why is this woman waking me up already?* I found out that while I was asleep, three weeks had passed.

Dr. Renoir came in later that morning, sat with me for a while chatting, checking my blood pressure and my eyes, still puffy with sleep. He asked me if I would welcome visitors. I could not think of who to welcome. He told me my mother had called a few times and asked if I was all right, if the sleep treatment was going as planned. I was intrigued by my mother's sudden interest, so I said yes.

In the ensuing days, I got up in the morning, had breakfast in my room, then I would go for walks in the park. The sky had turned cloudy and dark, never letting the sun through. The big old trees looked cold and extended leafless limbs toward the sky as if begging for the warmth of the sun. The grass had grown tall thanks to the rainfalls of the last few weeks.

It was a calm afternoon when my mother showed up at the clinic. I was sitting by the window, a book opened on my lap, daydreaming when she came in. It felt strange to see her here, visiting me. Normally, I was the one visiting her. Our roles were reversed; now, she was the guest, not me.

We exchanged meaningless kisses. She was dressed in her typical jersey clothes, expensive, of perfect quality, in a dull kind of way. She wore lifeless browns or beiges, a camel color wool coat, her lips carefully painted in the same coral color. The mass of her beautiful auburn hair was well managed with pins to keep it from floating wild. I had loved her hair so much as a small child when it was unruly.

When did my mother become so uniform, so ... robotic? When did she become passionless? Or had she always been like this, and I just had not noticed? I really wanted to love her, but I couldn't. I just couldn't. Not anymore.

I feel sad as I write this. I miss my mother now, miss what could have been, should have been, but never was. It wasn't my fault, but was it even hers?

She came to visit me a couple of times the following week, then stopped coming. I did not know why, and I did not really care. I was focused on myself, trying to imagine my new life back in the real world, beyond these bedroom walls. What would it be like to walk the streets again among strangers rushing, sheltered by heavy coats and black umbrellas? I also dreamed of the south, of Greece, of Israel, craving the sunlight on my skin, the warm sand under my feet, the endless iridescence of the Mediterranean Sea.

A week later, Dr. Renoir let me go. He insisted that I stay in touch, promising to help if I needed him. He wished me well, and we said our goodbyes. I packed in a minute, grabbed my coat, looked around the little room that had been my refuge, my shelter, and I promised myself to come back to see the trees budding in the spring. I closed the door behind me and started walking toward the exit.

Lost in my thoughts, I almost walked past without seeing her, but loud voices commanded my attention. I looked up to see my mother flanked on each side by male nurses. Her face was distorted by rage, and crude, graceless language was spilling out of her coral lips like water out of a broken faucet. I had never seen her like that. I stood there mesmerized for a minute or so, then walked back to the admission desk to find out what on earth my mother was doing here.

I found out that she had been admitted against her will and for the time being, she had been locked in a padded room. I asked permission to go and see her, as I was hoping that I might be able to calm her down. I was guided to another wing along an endless labyrinth of corridors I had never suspected existed. There were rows of closed doors, each with a small tempered glass window for observation.

The nurse stopped, pointing at a light green metal door. I approached slowly and peeked through its small glass pane. My mother was totally losing it. She looked like a trapped wild animal out of control, throwing herself against the walls, bouncing from one side to the other, screaming, although I could barely hear her voice through the heavy padding and the sound-proofed pane. Even if I had been allowed to, I would not have walked in. I had no idea who the woman in there was, and I don't think she would have recognized me. I turned to the nurse, who seemed embarrassed, as was I. She understood. We both stood there for a few more seconds, then she walked me back to the entrance.

~ REFLECTIONS & INSIGHTS ~

One of the most effective and exciting parts of the learning experience at the Primal Training Center was "Tape Review" when we, trainees, presented recorded sessions to the class under a senior therapist's supervision. Although it was at times a nerve-wracking experience for many, I came to value and enjoy these late-afternoon reviews. My work was often complimented, but this time there was something in France Janov's eyes. She looked at me without warmth, as though I was beneath her, and my therapy was somehow worthy of contempt.

I was triggered. Somehow it made me feel dirty. And ugly. As though she'd seen something disgusting. Then I remembered that I used to have nightmares that I looked like a hideous Picasso decomposed face, I'd wake up screaming.

Damien's face appeared in my memory with its habitual expression of distaste, his blue-gray eyes looking at me as though I was an unwelcome sight, a leper. I was crushed by a familiar flush of shame I so often felt in his presence. I wondered out loud: "Why do you hate me so much?"

But he was implacable as though the answer was self-evident. "Because you're a worm!" his eyes seemed to say.

Tears of humiliation squeezed from my eyes, and I dropped my gaze. "I'm sorry. I'm sorry I'm ugly! I'm so sorry ... "Tears were flowing freely now, my skin hot, quivering with self-disgust.

My distress increased as I remembered that look time after time through the years, each vignette provoking a new shudder of revulsion at myself and a fresh burst of tears.

The pain deepened as I began to plead, "Please ..." - which released a fresh storm, this time begging for him to find something, anything about me which was likeable. I went back to that time I overheard Damien's father admonishing him for treating me badly, which aroused floods of tears - somebody saw.

I looked at his face, it seemed softer somehow. This unleashed a storm of, "Please see something in me!" and "Please love me!" until I was spent.

A way to veil that shame was to be skinny, which was reinforced by the social milieux of the 1960s – by Twiggy, Jane Birkin, and the many anorexic-looking young women of those days. There was hope of acceptance in being slender. Whenever I happened to gain a few pounds, I felt miserable, hid under baggy clothes, and felt suicidal. My behavior back in the days came to mind, when I felt driven to sleep around because then I'd feel desired and "not ugly" for a while.

But much later, I found out that this need had its roots in my birth imprint - if I was thin enough, I could slip through and get born!

Since our emotional lives are built on the foundation of our imprint, thinness came to mean, by extension, that I would survive emotionally.

I have had variations of this feeling throughout my therapy. Each time, after re-living these moments, I feel as if I have slipped into a new body, a pleasurable sense of comfort spreads from cell to cell with each tear shed. And when I see my reflection in a mirror, I like the woman looking back at me.

And sometimes, I think I may never be free of this feeling, but as I keep revisiting those eyes, each time I connect the shame induced by his relentless attempts to break and humiliate me to its true context, I get relief.

Late in his life, Damien told me his behavior was payback for the time I rejected him when I was six years old and refused to let him spank me for making too much noise, while I screamed, "You have no right to touch me! You're not my father!"

I remember thinking how deranged it was to persecute a child for years for a single, trivial act of rebellion. His words did not bring me any comfort. It was too little too late.

I worked for Damien as a young adult back from my first year in Los Angeles; he would take me to lunch in nice restaurants. The way he looked at me outside of work made me feel awfully uncomfortable. He had the expression of a jilted lover. I wanted to believe it was my imagination playing tricks. But a few years later, right after my mother's funeral, Damien asked me with great intensity to lie down next to him.

I had no doubt then that he was inviting me to spend the night with him. I excused myself on the grounds that I was exhausted.

On my fiftieth birthday - and the anniversary of my mother's death - he visited me in Los Angeles. He took me, Peter, and Ken to our favorite hangout, A Votre Santé, where my wildlife photography was exhibited at the time. He must have noticed the friendship and warmth between us because he later remarked: "Those guys really care about you!" as if this was a difficult notion for him to grasp. I think it really disturbed him because oddly, during that visit he also remarked that the way he had treated me when I was little was a crime for which "they" should have locked him up and thrown away the key!

CHAPTER XXIV

Something Old.

Something New

OUT OF THE BLUE, Fabien, one of Damien's distant nephews, called me one evening to ask for a favor. I had met him on a couple of occasions when he was a cute little boy, and the Bivas clan had gathered for the yearly Jewish celebrations.

He was conducting a survey about customer satisfaction for well-known brands, a popular way for students to earn some extra money. It was for an auto brand. I knew nothing about cars and did not own one. I told him so, but he did not care, he just needed my name on the paperwork. We arranged to meet at my place the following evening.

When he showed up at my doorstep, I saw a tall and slim young man casually dressed in a corduroy jacket, his brown hair almost shoulder length. I had to make an effort to reconcile the memory of the boy I had met in childhood and the man standing in front of me, but then I recognized a childlike twinkle in his warm brown eyes. His face broke into an infectious smile. I led him to my sparsely furnished living room where we sat down across from each other at a long refectory table flanked with a bench on each side. We exchanged remarks about our new lives now as grown-ups. Then he opened his bag and pulled out an impressive stack of papers that he set on the table.

It took so long to work through each page that we stopped late in the evening, and Fabien asked if we could finish the next day. He showed up late the following afternoon and invited me to dinner at a local restaurant. Happy to go out, I took him up on his offer.

We drove to an eatery he knew well close by. Fabien opened the restaurant door and held it to let me in, like a real gentleman, which I found endearing. Inside, the small tables were covered with white tablecloths. Lit candles lights, small bouquets, and cutlery wrapped into white napkins made the place feel classy and quite romantic, not what I had expected. We chose an isolated table and sat down. He ordered a bottle of wine, which was served by a respectful *maître d'*. We savored our wine slowly.

There was a long, comfortable silence. We spoke up at the same time, curious to learn about each other. "You first!" I said with a smile, evading his question.

Fabien did not answer right away.

"My wife is having an affair with her boss," he said.

It surprised me. I thought they were happily married and very much in love.

I learned that soon after their honeymoon, Leah had gone to school to become a journalist and was now working for a well-known leftist paper. She felt she had married too young, and the journalistic world she was now a part of had tremendous appeal. Being gone for long hours and sometimes days at a time had taken its toll on their marriage, although it may have survived had she not become involved with another man, years older and married with children.

At first, he had hoped that the wounds could heal. But each time they attempted a reconciliation, anger and blame prevailed. Fabien filed for divorce, and she moved out. He asked me to keep this to myself, as he had not announced the divorce to his parents yet.

After our delicious meal, he drove me back home and walked me to my door. Before he left, we agreed to finish the survey the following day, same time, my place.

I realized that something unusual was happening to me. Since André had died, I felt I could never love again the way I had loved him. I had given André all I had, and there was nothing left in me. He had offered me a love so special that no other human being could ever come close to matching it. So, in the years that followed, while I traveled and went to university, I met men, but something was always missing in me or in them, and these passing adventures never amounted to more. But I had to admit that something about Fabien was very appealing to me, and for the first time since I had lost André, I found myself attracted to someone emotionally.

Did I have enough time to heal? Was there something special about this man I hardly knew? Was I sensing romantic feelings coming from him or was I just imagining them? I was beginning to feel this well-known but long buried sense of home next to him. He was kind, funny, open, and interesting. I felt I could trust him. I thought of him as someone who, once you had won his affection, was never going to betray it, someone like André perhaps.

I did not know how he felt about me, but what I did know was that he was still married and probably still in love with his wife. Regardless, I was amazed at the way I was beginning to feel again. I had not expected this to happen, ever. That night, I fell asleep smiling while picturing Fabien's face, happy that we were meeting again the following day.

OLD MEMORIES EMERGE

From that day forward, we met more often. It was so easy for us. We became involved, spent a lot of time together until Fabien asked me to move in with him.

Now living together, we settled into a comfortable and peaceful routine. I felt safe, at home, in the old apartment we had restored together with the help of his mom and dad. I loved the environment we had created. It had taken months and involved destroying walls, removing wallpaper, plastering, painting, tiling, installing shelves, and refinishing an old armoire that now stood imposingly against the white wall, lacquered in dark red that made it the focal point of the bedroom.

We had built a minuscule bathroom that could only be accessed through the narrow kitchen. A gigantic commercial laundry bucket now served as a small bathtub. Water splashed all over the floor when we showered, but I did not mind. I loved the colors, the textures, the white walls, the mattress on the carpeted floor. It was beautiful, peaceful, quiet, simple, and comfortable; a nest in which to grow in love and to build a life, a dream together.

Now, in bed I could hear him breathe lightly. He turned to his side and away from me, sound asleep. The sky was still dark, but now I was wide awake, so I decided to get up and go out for hot croissants fresh from the baker's oven. I would bring them back and make delicious coffee pressed with chicory just the way my grandmother always made it.

I got up, grabbed my jeans, T-shirt, and warm sweater, then quietly closed the bedroom door behind me. In the hallway, I put on my white sheepskin coat, slipped into warm boots, wrapped my woolen scarf around my neck twice and stepped out.

Outside it was bitterly cold. I turned left, toward the bakery closest to us. The cold felt good, my skin came to life, my eyes were wide open, and my cheeks were turning pink from the increased blood flow. The wind was forcing my legs into long strides. There was no one on the street at this time of day. I arrived at the bakery but there were no inviting warm yellow lights, no delicious smells of hot bread. It was closed.

I retraced my steps and started down our narrow street towards another bakery we sometimes went to. I picked up the pace as I wanted to get back before Fabien got up. *It'll be nice to surprise him*, I thought smiling.

Ten minutes later I walked into the warmth of the brightly lit store, the air heavy with the aromas of freshly baked bread and colorful cakes. Preoccupied by the thought that Fabien might be up already, I walked straight to the counter, asked for the croissants, paid, and quickly left. I was growing nervous for no reason I could fathom.

I started to move faster and as I did, I imagined a threatening, malevolent presence behind me. I could almost hear its heavy footsteps despite the muffling carpet of snow, I could almost feel its hot and humid breath on the back of my neck. Something came alive in the pit of my stomach. Now, all I could hear was the beat of my heart. I began to run, but "it" was coming for me, catching up with me, sliding along the curb at the speed of a snake, like the one I had seen as a child on a mountain hike, one moment bathing in the sun, then gone in the blink of an eye.

I could not outrun it, and I could not turn around. I imagined a sharp knife held up high in the air, coming down to stab me between the shoulder blades, almost touching, almost cutting. My heart felt like it was going to explode, making me want to fall to the ground and curl up in a little ball, disappear, melt away, or fall on my knees and beg, beg for mercy. Inside, I was pleading, promising, bargaining. *"Please, please don't hurt me! I'll do anything, I swear. Please stop!"* It kept playing endlessly like a mantra as if it had the power to delay the final fatal blow for a second or two or three.

My hands pressed on my stomach, I reached our building. I climbed the stairs four steps at a time, made it to our landing, banged loudly on the door, no time to find my key, my whole body shaking.

With his long hair disheveled, Fabien opened the door. I could see an expression of surprise on his kind face. "What's going on?" he asked. I could see that he was looking *at* me, not *past* me.

I turned around. I was alone on the landing, no one was climbing the stairs behind me. Without answering, I pushed past him, turned around, slammed the door shut, and like a rag doll, I collapsed onto the floor shaking and sobbing uncontrollably.

Fabien did not even need to know what had shaken me up so badly. He sat down on the floor next to me, his back leaning against the wall, and reached out for my icy hand. He held it, instilling his natural calm and warmth. I began to tell him what had happened out there, my voice still shaking. In the street, I had to run, run, run as fast as I could. But there was no one after me, no snake, no monster, no knife ready to stab my flesh, no one breathing down my neck. So what was I running from?

As I had learned and trained myself what to do during these episodes of panic that had become all too frequent, I began to retrace my steps out loud, recounting what had happened, where, when, how, with whom, until my mind was able to grasp at something sketchy that became clearer as the events unfolded, until I could make some sense of it all.

So, in my mind, I walked back to the shop. There was the woman who handed me the croissants. She reminded me of someone. I painted a picture of a stocky, imposing woman, wearing a long white apron and a cold expression on her face. She had small, beady eyes and a smile that did not reach them.

Then, from the corner of my eye, on the left, I could see a shadowy figure, almost ghostlike, transparent but a presence that could not be ignored. A man had been in the shop, but I had not paid much attention to him. Amid waves of fear, hurt, and the sadness of immeasurable loss, I remembered something forgotten. I saw Madame Valcourt, my brutal and abusive foster mother, whose physical features were so much like those of the woman in the shop, and Mr. Valcourt, whose very existence I had erased from my mind until that morning. To my surprise, I felt he had always been there somewhere in the corner of my mind, but amnesia had blocked all memories of him until then.

Still on the floor, almost completely curled up within the protective shell of Fabien's body, sobbing without restraint, my mind was flooded with images of the past, my brain beginning to make some sense out of this physiological and emotional chaos. Something was pushing from within that wanted to see the light of day, something that I could no longer ignore. It wouldn't stop until I made room for it and validated its reality.

*

After we had settled in, I decided to look for work and it did not take too long before an exciting opportunity presented itself. The work consisted of helping a writer brainstorm, organize, and edit the manuscript he was working on. We had a promising phone conversation, and I was thrilled at the prospect of an exciting job. We set up a time to meet at his place.

On the day of the appointment, I took the subway train and arrived at my destination. As I was walking, I remember looking at the pavement intensely and watching myself put one foot in front of the other. I had to slow down my pace because each step that brought me closer to the "job" triggered anxiety and, with a few more steps, panic. The growing terror was like a wall I kept bumping into.

I experimented by taking one step backward, then another, and another. The terror diminished enough that I attempted to take a few steps forward. Panic increased until I bumped into that wall of terror again. I felt dizzy. I repeated the backward and forward steps a few times until I realized I would not make it. I had to give up.

Finally, I turned around and went back home. On the way back, palpable relief gave way to despair and unbearable self-loathing. I was a useless wimp for giving up and hated myself for not pushing through.

~ REFLECTIONS & INSIGHTS ~

After a year in therapy in Los Angeles, California, I returned to Paris with Kenneth, my American husband. Ken did not speak the language, so he began attending French classes at the Alliance Française. In the meantime, I was the one who had to go to work and earn a living. I found a job as a receptionist at a fashion magazine called *Biba*.

We lived in my brother's small apartment in the 18th arrondissement while my job was somewhere south, in the 15th arrondissement. I used to walk to and from my job, a 45-minute walk through the most beautiful districts and neighborhoods of my hometown, each time crossing the magnificent Pont Alexandre III over the Seine.

Each day as I woke up, devastation crept in, along with exhaustion and the conviction that I was incapable of leaving the apartment, let alone getting to work and spending the day there. The moment I lay down in our tiny, soundproof room, Ken by my side, intense sadness and despair would take over and buckets of tears would cascade out of me. Every so often Ken would put his hand gently over my head, like adults do when they console a little child. This would trigger deeper tears of desperation I felt would never end. Warmth and kindness and strength emanated from Ken. I trusted him without reservation.

And then, I would be done. I would get out of the "Primal box," rinse my face with cold water and leave, ready to face the day. I felt relief and pleasure brought on by a sense of deep connection to the outside world. Colors, scents, and touch felt much more intense, triggering deeply pleasurable sensations and feelings.

I had been my stepfather's slave for many years, feeling worthless, undeserving of love and care. It had made earning a living an unattainable goal. As a young adult before therapy, it had been impossible for me to work for more than a few weeks at a time at dead-end low paying jobs. With no access to my childhood pain, the despair and the terror that came over me when I tried to do meaningful well-paid work had been it so far impossible.

But now, I had to make a good living, especially since Ken depended on me.

Over the next few weeks, I had to revisit those feelings over and again, peeling away layer after layer. In doing so, I became acutely aware of how being dysfunctional had served to keep those ugly feelings of undeserving worthlessness at bay.

One day at a time, I became stronger. I had made it through another day, I had unflinching love and support from Ken, and I was feeling alive and filled with joy as I walked across Paris, enjoying the architecture, the history, and the beauty I saw everywhere. These were treats that regaled all my senses. I was safe, at home, and cherished, which gave me the strength to let the suffering of my days around Damien gradually recede.

Primal is not a process that takes care of itself. To succeed, we have to feel, connect, realize, and use our insights to "terminate" behaviors that are detrimental to our well-being and to change our lives; it is an unending dance between *feeling* and *doing*. Without the *doing* part of the process, we cannot access the deeper layers of Pain of that same *feeling* instilled in us over many years. But new tears give more relief, and as we get stronger, new steps change us. This allows deeper access to the Pain, and the cycle goes on until we are no longer triggered. These last conscious steps of choosing to change our behavior are essential for the Primal process to be complete and for our lives to really change.

~ REFLECTIONS & INSIGHTS ~

In 1987, I was 36 years old. The night before my therapy session, I was falling asleep when troubling memories of an event that took place ten years earlier crossed my mind, it was on a winter morning, when I had re-discovered the existence of Monsieur Valcourt, of whom I had erased all memories.

The disturbing thoughts were still there in the morning, annoying, like an irritating tune that would not stop playing in my head. When Maya, my therapist, asked me how I was, I hesitated, then replied I would feel better if the nagging thoughts in my head could just stop.

"What thoughts?" she asked.

Reluctantly, I began to recount the events that took place on a pitch-dark winter morning, which led me to remember the existence of Monsieur Valcourt.

"Why did I forget that he was there?" I exclaimed.

Ignoring my question, Maya inquired, "Tell me more about him."

I felt a chill crawling up my spine, a sense of danger, a need to run. I tried to stay calm and fight the creepy sensation, but my heart began racing as if I was running.

"I'm scared," I said, feeling miserable and small, my hands on my heart as if to slow it down. My body felt colder now.

"What does it feel like ... to be scared?"

I'm alone on the street, no one knows I'm here. I'm cold. I'm alone.

I wanted to hang on to something, someone. But who? Fabien, my boyfriend at the time? Or Monsieur Valcourt? I thought about that for a moment, that strange association, endeavoring to pierce the veil of time. I told Maya about the ghost-like man in my foster home that frightened me and attracted me all at once.

"He feels ... faded. He is somehow in the background, 'effacé' is the French word, and gentle ... I think."

"Gentle?" Maya echoed.

"Yes, kind and frail, and old, I think." *My own* words took me by surprise, until then, Monsieur Valcourt had been erased from my conscious mind. But suddenly, he appeared next to me, wiping blood off my face with a soft white cloth.

Before I could stop myself, I sat up. I had just seen an angry face right in front of me, red, ugly, terrifying. I was in danger, I felt cornered. I had to get out.

"What happened?" Maya inquired.

Miserable, I said, "It's her." Suddenly, I could not speak. I froze, felt cold despite the warmth in the air. I was choking on something. I was sure I was going to stop breathing. *I'm finished, I thought.*

Maya put a hand on my shoulder for a few seconds, long enough for me to take in the warmth I ached for. And then I broke down into a million tiny pieces. The veil turned to mist, evaporated, and Madame Valcourt came into sharp focus. She was big, her face dark red with rage, her eyes cold as a snake's. Her gray hair up, her lips thin and tight. Just like she had been in that kitchen decades ago.

The terror took over, spreading ice down my bloodstream. I felt my body shaking and curled up on the mattress, possessed by frantic serpentine movements I was not able to stop. They felt so ... liberating, full of a rage that grew more powerful as my legs were pushing and kicking. I heard the switch to rhythmic breaths that seemed to go on and on. Hyperventilation would get me dizzy within seconds; it would be unsustainable, and yet, right now, it felt so natural, there was no other way until it would pass, and the tears would come back, deep, rough, heart-wrenching, tearing me inside. I could hear the sound of my voice when my vocal cords opened up; it was that of a small child, and then a baby, and again a small child.

Then I sat up, back in the room with my therapist. I was shaken up; my mind was present now, but my body was not quite back just yet, still vulnerable, too open.

I recounted what had happened down in the rabbit hole, that time when Madame Valcourt had punched me in the nose. I felt an empowering rage as I pushed and kicked, and such immense sadness and devastation as Monsieur Valcourt was cleaning me up, in the aftermath of that day. The blow had come out of the blue with no warning, no signal to run. I kept feeling my nose, sensing a touch of discomfort, not pain really, but at the edge of it. Maya looked at me with kind eyes, and I felt my throat close up again. She saw the change in me.

"What just happened?" she asked.

"The fear …," I said.

She remained quiet, waiting for more.

"Your eyes, they're kind …" I burst into tears, in deep long, cleansing adult sobs, then crossing lines into the same long childhood sobs, and back. The immensity of the sorrow was overflowing.

Another scene crossed my mind. It was around the same time, a scene of terror and the soothing power of unexpected kindness. I was in Paris, on a subway train ride, sitting down, trying to read a book I could not focus on, impatient to get out of this crowded, overheated space full of strangers, when a woman walked in and sat down across from me. I felt an instant connection to her. She was stunning. She had coppery blond hair flattering her slightly tanned face, and her eyes were green and bright. I was struck by her expression of kindness and humanity. I was mesmerized. I was trying to remain discreet but failed. I could not take my eyes off her.

She looked away, then looked at me, a radiant smile across her face. I smiled back feeling shy. A few stations later, she got up and stepped out onto the platform as the train doors closed in a whoosh. Panic struck like lightning, my senses on high alert. *I'm going to die! I must get out, I must get out, now!!!*

It seemed an eternity before the train stopped at the next station. I ran out the door with no idea where I was, just knowing beyond any doubt that I had to run, my life depended on it. People were coming from all directions, the crowd closing in on me. I aimed for the white tiled wall by a bench, bent over holding my stomach, trying to breathe. I thought I was going to die right there and then in plain sight.

The rushing wave was passing me by, strangers throwing glances of indifference or dislike at the sight of yet another drunk or junkie. Terror was invisible to them; I was lost in that human herd.

I opened my eyes when out of the crowd came the sweet voice of a little old lady. "Are you alright dear? Do you need help?" she asked.

I looked up at her, so grateful for this human being standing next to me. Hanging on to the back of the bench, I rose and steadied myself, still holding my stomach, forced to bend slightly to breathe easier. I told her I was scared and asked her if she would walk me home. "Of course!" she replied.

We climbed up the subway stairs and walked together slowly, huddled together like an old couple. I lived a few streets away. She left me at my door after making sure that I was going to be okay. By then the panic had run its course. I was just worn out and weak. I told her how grateful I was for her kindness, and we parted ways. It would be years before I understood that the woman's coppery blond hair evoked the devastating memory of my mother's long dark red hair.

*

Maya had shown genuine curiosity. She was there, she was listening. Her presence gave me a sense of safety, emphasized by her questions, her silences, her touch. That was the dialectic I needed to let the gates open, the very opposite of how I was treated as a child. Memories separated by time and space returned to me, released by the same need for kindness and protection.

Maya, Monsieur Valcourt, Fabien, the beautiful lady in the subway train, the sweet old lady who walked me home that day, had all offered the humanity I had craved as a small child.

During those years of abuse, there was nowhere to run or hide, no protection or hope and no expiration date. But I looked for an anchor at all costs, and I found it in the colors of nature so bright after the tears, the roughness of a tree bark under my palms, and the sounds of creatures that lived in the grasses. It was a time of truce, and their tranquil presence a soothing interlude.

I believe I learned instinctively to take comfort in the sweet memories of early childhood with my father and then with Madame Pomaré, the angel who took care of me until I was two years old. Both instilled in me the priceless experience of affection and tenderness. Just as "fight or flight" is our response to threat and unpleasantness, the "relaxation response" is the parasympathetic nervous system's reaction to kindness and love, a learned response essential to our healthy development.

I came to understand why bodily sensations terrified me so much, why they made me feel like I was in mortal danger. Madame Valcourt had been brutal, violent, sadistic, sudden, and unpredictable. So were the panic attacks.

I realized that panic attacks were memories re-experienced out of their original context. The fear belonged somewhere in the past, out of reach, unconscious. The abuse was horrific at times so when consciousness returned, it was in installments, a moment at a time, as I got stronger and able to allow more to surface.

Little by little, I understood why my first line of defense against panic was to freeze. Being immobile, almost catatonic deprived Madame Valcourt of the thrill that she felt when inflicting pain, and she would lose interest.

But when full-blown terror and the violent shaking could no longer be repressed, when my heart was about to explode, my throat closing up, I had to run, I just had to! That was my second line of defense, to run like the wind. Nothing could stop me. The fact that there was nowhere to run did not make one bit of a difference - the fight or flight reaction demands one or the other, or sometimes both.

THE GIFT OF DIALECTIC

During one of our didactic classes at the Primal Training Center, Art explained his concept of dialectic in Primal Therapy with an anecdote about an amoeba that exemplified how dialectic heals by causing repression to fail. It went as follows: an amoeba is floating in water with Indian ink, which is a threat to its survival. To protect itself, the amoeba encapsulates the ink until it finds itself floating in clear water. The danger has passed. Then - in this safe environment - the ink capsules move to the cell's membrane, open, and release the ink in the clear water. So, Art took the word *dialectic* and gave it his own meaning of the 'antidote to pain' which makes it possible for Pain to be released.

The point was that neurosis works much in the same way. When the hurt inflicted upon us reaches a threshold that is a threat to our survival and our sanity, as children we "encapsulate" the memories in our unconscious. Repression will last until we find ourselves in an emotionally safe environment. Thus, the role of the therapist is to provide an environment we trust and build a relationship based on respect, good listening skills, genuine curiosity, kindness, and empathy.

As time goes by, defenses begin to crumble. Repressed pain pushes to be released; Primal Pain is expressed when we relive what it was like not to be loved, when we cry it out to exhaustion, and finally beg for what we needed so desperately but were then prevented from expressing. The primal experience ends with integration when the emotions and the memories uncovered come together and result in insights that show what drove a specific neurotic behavior of ours. Art taught us that once free of the need for repression, defenses just disappear. That lesson stayed with me because of its simplicity and clarity about what makes us neurotic and how to recover and heal.

So when the memory of Monsieur Valcourt came back to me in the primal I had that day, I realized that as I had spent more time with Fabien and as we had grown close, his love and genuine kindness, his desire to understand, the way he looked at me, stood by me, never judging, never doubting was the clear water, the dialectic that let repressed memories come back to me. After the years since André had died, he was the first person to come into my life and re-offer what had been lost: the safe environment that made it possible for the unconscious pain to reveal itself.

CHAPTER XXV

Leaving France

FOR YEARS, I had been looking for someone who would acknowledge the reality of my condition and help me make sense of what was happening to me. When I came across *The Primal Scream*, it was with shock and excitement that I found passages about panic attacks. In his book, Art wrote that they could be treated successfully in Primal therapy.

I found out that the institute where I could get treated was in Los Angeles, California. At that point, leaving home on a daily basis was a trying experience for me; I feared the streets, the open air, and the crowds. So how could I cross an ocean? However, I felt I had no other choice. I decided I would go to America even if it was the last thing I did.

We drove from Paris to Le Havre, where I was going to board a Russian boat called *The Lermontov* for the transatlantic crossing. Reine, Damien, Adam, and Fabien came along to see me off. There was a lot of warmth, and even my parents looked genuinely sad to see me go. Or was I misreading their expressions? Perhaps they were reminded of past separations.

We walked a long way from the parking lot to the large hall where officials checked my passport and ticket. Then we sat there on a bench waiting for the loudspeakers to announce that it was time to board. No one other than travelers were allowed on the ship, so when the warning finally came through, my family walked with me to the bottom of the stairs that lead to the deck. We spent a few minutes hugging and kissing.

"Take good care of yourself, don't forget us, come back to us," said Reine. These were words I had needed to hear my whole life.

My brother said nothing but gave me a heartfelt hug. Letting go of him felt like something had torn inside.

It was time to go. What had been set in motion could not be undone, so I climbed the stairs to the deck where I was welcomed by the members of the Russian crew. Once up there, I went to look down and I spotted my family. The ship was already moving along the pier and gradually getting away from it. As I was being taken away from all I had ever known, I felt a strange mix of emotions. I wanted to stay, but I wanted to go; I was sad and thrilled all at once.

Then I saw my brother break loose from their small group and start running along the ship. He was running faster and faster, all the while looking at me and waving. His entire body language, the expression on his face, his waving was not saying goodbye. It was saying, "Please, don't go."

Suddenly, everything in me wanted to stop the ship, run to him, hold him, and promise never to leave.

I saw my brother's silhouette getting smaller and smaller in the distance. He had reached the end of the pier, and he was just standing there. Tears were running down my cheek. As the pier got further and further away, my brother became like a little dot in the distance.

It was a long journey, seven days and seven nights to cross the Atlantic Ocean. I spent a lot of time on deck, watching the ocean and the sea life – dolphins, whales, and other creatures of the sea – that were following the ship. I was there at sunset and at sunrise every day. I could have stared at the beautiful starry sky in delight forever. Nowhere else could one witness the infinite number of stars in the distance, some so faint they could only be guessed at, some closer and twinkling as if sending a friendly sign. Sometimes I felt I could almost touch them. The sky was everywhere, meeting the horizon in every direction. It made me feel like I was connected to the vast expanse of sky, ocean, and earth, a minuscule but important part of all that existed in this world.

I will never forget the first time I saw the land of the American continent appear in the distance. The vision was so faint that it almost appeared to be a figment of my imagination. Fascination kept me glued to the railing, watching intently.

It was still dark, but the sky was turning from black into the deepest shade of blue. I could see some light from the east where a trail of orangey pink clouds floated high in the sky. The blurred details of the land became more distinct. My eyes were drawn to the Statue of Liberty in its turquoise, teal, and golden splendor. The entire city was now crystal clear as the sun was rising. Tall, slender buildings were like giants effortlessly touching the sky. The sight appeared unreal, more like a science fiction fantasy to the European in me.

The piers got closer and closer, and our ship maneuvered to approach one of them. It was exciting and a bit scary too. As we approached the pier, and the ship came to a halt, the engines stopped. The noises of New York surrounded us; people were screaming on the docks, attempting to be heard from a distance above the noise of cars, trucks, and sirens. Here I was, ready for a new adventure, a new chapter, a new life.

The End

Appendix

II

Primal Therapy Done Right

The mysteries of the unconscious mind have long captivated human curiosity, transcending time, and cultural boundaries. The unconscious can be pictured as a vault where our past physical and emotional traumas are archived, forgotten experiences too agonizing to integrate when they initially occurred. A key to this vault is the therapeutic approach of Primal therapy.

Repression of Traumatic Events Often Begins at Birth

In his book, "Birth without Violence" (1974), Frédérick Leboyer, a French obstetrician advocated for a gentler approach to childbirth. He believed the practice of modern medicalized birth to be a series of traumatic events for the newborns and describes the unnecessary agony and suffering they experience.

He proposed the use of gentle methods to ease the newborn's transition from the womb to the outside world by creating a darker, peaceful environment during delivery and by placing the baby on the mother's stomach immediately after birth - as well as delay the cutting of the umbilical cord, infant massage, and a warm bath.

Laying the baby on the mother's stomach allows the infant to listen to a familiar heartbeat and remember the womb. Delaying the cutting of the umbilical cord allows the baby time to adjust to breathing with his lungs and prevents shock from the sudden lack of umbilical cord oxygen. Infant massage is meant to recreate the wave-like movement in the womb and a warm bath mimics the weightless feelings from early embryonic development. All of Leboyer's practices strive to avoid trauma to the newborn, and ensure a gentle, nurturing start to life.

Pre-Verbal & Emotional Repression

According to Dr. Janov, at birth, our memories are encoded as sensations, forming the "first line" of consciousness. Emotional wounds develop later, etching into the limbic system—the "second line" of consciousness. When children face trauma and neglect, the resulting pain is often repressed, leading to a disconnection from part of the self and resulting in lifelong emotional struggles.

This repression creates a protective amnesia, disrupting normal brain function. The dislocation of function caused by neurosis is like a mass of entangled wires, some unplugged and some plugged in, but in the wrong sockets. After the feeling experience of a Primal, some of these wires have been finally plugged in or re-plugged into the right sockets so that now, the electrical and chemical currents can move freely delivering information to every single cell via the re-established and now functional synapses and free flowing neurotransmitters. From this perspective, amnesia begins at the precise moment that the wires were unplugged, interrupting the flow of information that would have kept our memory intact.

Primal therapy seeks to reconnect these neural pathways, allowing for the resolution of repressed traumas.

"Dialectic" in Primal Therapy

Accessing past trauma requires the patient to feel safe through what Dr. Janov termed "dialectic." It is an unfortunate choice of word since "dialectic" has meant different things to different people. Hegel used the term "Dialectics" to describe a method of philosophical argument that involves a contradictory process between opposing sides.

Janov's term "dialectic" refers to what counteracts the deprivation that we experienced in childhood - love, touch, understanding, warmth, being listened to, being valued, and so forth. Dialectic here means the "met need" in opposition to the "unmet need."

He explained his concept of dialectic in Primal Therapy with an anecdote about an amoeba that exemplified how dialectic heals by causing repression to fail. The amoeba is floating in water contaminated with Indian ink, a threat to its survival. To protect itself, the amoeba encapsulates the ink until it finds itself floating in clear water. The danger has now passed. Then - in this safe environment - the ink capsules move to the cell's membrane, open, and release the ink in the clear water.

His point was that neurosis works much in the same way. When the hurt inflicted upon us reaches a threshold that is a threat to our survival and our sanity, as children we "encapsulate" the memories in our unconscious.

Establishing Trust

Being given the nurturing care that we did not receive causes stress cracks in the dam of our defense system, leading to the breakdown of defenses and the natural need to release repressed pain, The therapeutic relationship hinges on trust. The therapist is genuinely empathetic and compassionate, and above all, listens to and explores with the patient the underlying motivations in what is expressed, as well as encourages him to follow the tears (or the anger that often precedes the tears).

When therapy is done right, the process of opening up happens naturally in sessions, when the patient is ready. Extended periods of social isolation, deprivation and verbal provocation intended to break down psychological defenses are unnecessary measures that made it difficult if not impossible for the patient to feel safe for very long, if at all. Forcing the breakdown of defenses is a mistake because it will damage the patient-therapist relationship.

Transference Matters

Transference reveals important aspects of a patient's traumatic history and of how it manifests in the present. And neglecting the significance of transference can be very detrimental to the therapy because it goes against the very basic necessity of establishing trust.

The patient might attribute traits, and feelings to his therapist, interpreting a behavior, a tone of voice, a look, a gesture, in a positive or negative way that has reminded him of the people he interacted with during his formative years. Exploring these projections can be extremely valuable.

Beyond that, disregarding transference is a mistake because it bypasses the present. The feelings a patient has towards his therapist, at any given time, might be where the trigger is, as is the access to his underlying hurt. Exploring these emotions in the session is paramount for the patient to trust.

The Primal Approach

Primal therapy is about hearing the underlying pain and meeting the unmet need that caused the hurt in the first place, but it is equally important for the therapist to be open to discuss and explore present issues, as discussed above.

In practice, primal therapy meets a patient where he is at. If a patient begins to tear, the therapist does not ask "Why are you crying?" because he is already in the feeling emerging from right brain with limited language skills. Answering such a question could activate the rational left brain and rob him of his feeling experience.

However, flexibility is key, and for every rule there are exceptions. In the case of a patient who has spent years crying out his distress as a child without being seen, acknowledged, or comforted, the question and the tone in which it is asked may well be the one intervention that leads him to the connected feeling, while no inquiry from the therapist could be interpreted as a lack of interest, recreating his past and resulting in the shutdown of his feeling.

The primal therapist listens for triggers, a trigger being something that causes an emotional reaction - a scene in a movie, a song, or anything where the smooth flow of consciousness is disrupted by distress.

But a trigger is really *anything* that interrupts that smooth flow of consciousness. Sometimes access to primal feelings is facilitated by focusing on positive memories rather than painful experiences past or present.

Just like when we are being born, we need time, we need to move at our own pace, in a safe, non-threatening environment, and with the presence of a warm, compassionate, and curious therapist to go down that road less traveled that will take us to where the agony of our traumatic past resides.

We are going back in time in a real sense. Once there, we fully react to the hurt that was buried for so long. The healing begins when we fully react to the pain, when our entire body is in the feeling experience, and we express now what we could not then, with our tears, our screams, our words, when we reach the depth of our rage and our despair.

Our voice switches to the crying of the tiny baby or the little boy or girl. Once at a retreat in the South of France, a patient cried through an entire group session, in near darkness. Later, in post group, patients commented that they could have sworn a baby was born that night, in that group room. We are reconnecting to something from a time long gone but that lives on forever in our every cell.

It is like elucidating a mystery that had so far remained unsolved.

In summary, when our needs in childhood go unmet, we experience psychological pain. Beyond a certain intensity, this pain gives rise to repression and becomes primal pain. This disorders our thought processes and gives power to our defense mechanisms. We now deny, project and rationalize, which in turn leads to maladaptive behaviors we call act-outs that keep our pain unconscious.

The pain that drives our neurotic impulses has become embedded in our physiology. This is why we are helpless to change, regardless of how much we think, analyze, and try to overcome a disserving behavior. For the behavior to change, a connection needs to be made between our intellectual desire and the physiology that has locked us up in an unconscious emotional prison.

Integration in Primal Therapy

After a feeling experience, the focus moves from catharsis to integration. What was re-lived in a session is processed to allow integration of what was uncovered and is now conscious. Often, we are filled with insights, in the form of "That's why I always ..." statements.

Integration is an essential part of Primal therapy, the most important part of a session. It shocks, it delights, it may even be a euphoric experience. It is the healing equation without which no real and long-lasting resolution is possible. Done right, it gives us the tools we need to end the protective maladaptive behaviors we no longer need.

Integration happens at the end of the feeling experience; we are silently processing what we relived. The importance of a post-session can never be overestimated. It is then that we verbalize and share with the therapist what we went through and the insights we gained that tie our present behaviors to our past traumas. The therapist will explore with the patient which steps need to be taken to break a lifelong behavior that had become second nature.

*

The realizations we have in therapy forever change our perception of our *self* and of the world. Pain no longer colors and distorts our perceptions and beliefs.

To be true to our new sense of self, we will now have to act on our changed perception of reality. After a lifetime in the grip of neurosis, it is an important part of the therapeutic process to explore ways to adjust to this new reality by taking steps and making choices that will improve our lives. Wellbeing is now within reach.

Change does not happen overnight, but rather incrementally by taking baby steps as we continue to work with our emotions until they no longer govern the way we feel, think and act. By systematically confronting the old pain inflicted upon us, we begin to regain compassion for ourselves and the people in our lives, with a greater ability to feel connected in warm and intimate relationships.

Healing the Therapist

The working principle in Primal therapy is that the therapist cannot take patients through issues that they have not resolved themselves. Therefore, it is essential for the therapist to have worked through most of their own main issues and to be continuously engaged in revisiting and resolving painful psychological challenges they encounter as they get triggered in their practice and in their lives. If not, poor interventions are unavoidable, especially in a therapy as technique poor as Primal therapy where therapeutic moves are based almost entirely on intuition and instinct. When a therapist's pain is triggered, it manifests as poor interventions to the detriment of the patient, and, if prolonged, to the detriment of their therapy.

Additionally, when the therapist is defending against his own psychological pain, the patient's unconscious will sense that, and avoid that pain within himself. Therefore, it is paramount for the therapist to make sure that it is not his unconscious bias that is driving the interventions, but the pure and clean intuition born of his deep insights.

Supervision is Essential

Recording and reviewing sessions and working with peers will allow the therapist to gain insight into their own practice and identify areas where they may have missed important cues or made inappropriate interventions.

It is essential to maintain the quality and integrity of the therapy. It provides the therapist with valuable feedback, helps identify blind spots, ensures the ethical practice of the therapy, and promotes ongoing personal and professional growth,

Primary Track, Secondary Track, & Abreaction

Whatever the story, wherever the trigger, the right track will always take the patient by surprise. This feature is unique to Primal therapy. It is how the therapist knows that the patient is on the primary track. It is the therapist's job to make sure that the patient is on the primary track. A common mistake is for the therapist to be overly focused on the patient's past and to make moves that take him out of the present and push him into the past prematurely.

The patient must be given the space and the time to talk about what is troubling him. This is a time when the therapist's curiosity really matters. His open-ended questions will encourage the patient to describe a feeling, a moment, a memory, in descriptive details that will guide him to the buried hurt. As he gets close, his voice might break, his body language change.

Feeling on a secondary track is a form of *abreaction* that is difficult to recognize because it can be moving.

Although abreaction is easily identifiable because it does not touch or move us, when a patient is on a secondary track, he might feel deeply, *but* at the end of the session, he will not experience any satisfactory resolution, because important steps were skipped, and something essential was avoided at the beginning of the session.

The secondary track can be the primary track, but the underlying feeling has not been accessed at its point of origin. It is like entering the feeling through a side door rather than through the main entrance door. As a result, important connections from the present will not be made, and the patient will not be able to link his present issues and behaviors to the past hurt. The result will be a lack of insights. This is one of the biggest mistakes made in the practice of Primal therapy because it disrupts its natural progression, derailing the feeling process off its tracks.

Consequently, the patient might spend many sessions, if not many years, going over the same issues without getting long term relief and resolution. Eventually, he might end the therapy and walk away convinced that it is he who has failed, or that he is too difficult a case.

Primal therapy is a learning process that takes time to master. However, it should not take years to yield results. If it does, it is likely to be caused by ineffective therapy rather than the complexities of the patient's neurosis.

Monitoring a Patient's Progress

Monitoring a patient's progress involves jointly evaluating their wellbeing and their behavior in the outside world. Are they achieving the goals set at the beginning of the therapy, or are they making strides towards these goals? This provides an opportunity for both the patient and the therapist to discuss the patient's current progress or difficulties in both real-life situations and during therapy sessions. It is also a good time to address any misconception the patient may have about the therapeutic process. Patients are encouraged to maintain a journal to track their insights.

Success in Primal Therapy

The success of Primal therapy lies in tangible life changes, better health choices, emotional resilience, fulfilling relationships. The patient will emerge empowered to meet his own needs and pursue his goals in life.

He is now in the driver's seat, a true adult, taking responsibility for his own destiny.

More information about Michelle's work can be found at

IntegratedPrimal.com